THE PENGUIN BOOK OF ALL-NEW AUSTRALIAN JOKES

Phillip Adams, a newspaper columnist for 45 years, re-energised the Australian film industry, producing a dozen features (from *The Adventures of Barry McKenzie* to *We of the Never Never*) and chairing the Australian Film Commission, the Commission for the Future and other bodies too numerous to mention. Addicted to collecting (everything from Egyptian mummies to jokes), he presents *Late Night Live* for ABC Radio National.

After dancing with Humphrey B. Bear in Adelaide, **Patrice Newell** modelled in Chicago, acted in soaps in New York, worked as a researcher for the Seven Network, presented news and current affairs programs for SBS and cohosted the Nine Network's *Today* show. These days she runs a large cattle property and plants olive groves whilst managing a small daughter and Phillip Adams.

Other collections by
Phillip Adams and Patrice Newell

The Penguin Book of Australian Jokes
The Penguin Book of More Australian Jokes
The Penguin Book of Jokes from Cyberspace
The Penguin Book of Schoolyard Jokes
Pocket Jokes
What a Joke!
What a Giggle!

THE PENGUIN BOOK OF

ALL-NEW

AUSTRALIAN

JOKES

*Collected by Phillip Adams
and Patrice Newell*

PENGUIN BOOKS

Penguin Books Australia Ltd
487 Maroondah Highway, PO Box 257
Ringwood, Victoria 3134, Australia
Penguin Books Ltd
Harmondsworth, Middlesex, England
Penguin Putnam Inc.
375 Hudson Street, New York, New York 10014, USA
Penguin Books Canada Limited
10 Alcorn Avenue, Toronto, Ontario, Canada M4V 3B2
Penguin Books (N.Z.) Ltd
Cnr Rosedale and Airborne Roads, Albany, Auckland, New Zealand
Penguin Books (South Africa) (Pty) Ltd
5 Watkins Street, Denver Ext 4, 2094, South Africa
Penguin Books India (P) Ltd
11, Community Centre, Panchsheel Park, New Delhi 110 017, India

First published by Penguin Books Australia Ltd 2000

10 9 8 7 6 5 4 3 2 1

Designed by Erika Budiman, Penguin Design Studio
Cover illustration by Ned Culic
Typeset in Stempel Garamond 11.5/18pt by Midland Typesetters,
Maryborough, Victoria
Printed in Australia by Australian Print Group, Maryborough, Victoria

National Library of Australia
Cataloguing-in-Publication data:

The Penguin book of all-new Australian jokes.
  Includes index.
  ISBN 0 14 029058 3.

  1. Australian wit and humor. I. Adams, Phillip, 1939– . II. Newell,
  Patrice, 1956– . III. Title: All-new Australian jokes.

A828.02

www.penguin.com.au

ACKNOWLEDGEMENTS

We would like to thank our countless collaborators – the hundreds of hunter-gatherers who send us jokes from all over the country. Foremost amongst them are Alex Selles, our IT expert, and the indefatigable Christian Raith.

CONTENTS

Acknowledgements...v

Introduction 1

A

Anzac Spirit... 12

Australian Limericks..................................... 16

Aviation 18

Azaria 19

B

Babes & Sucklings..................................... 22

Bars, Beer & Blokes 34

Blonde Bombshells...................................... 56

Bumper Stickers 67

Business Advice 75

C

'Twas the Night Before Christmas............................. 94

All Creatures Great & Small 105

D

Dad & Dave & Mabel 122

E

Terms of Employment...............................130

F

Fairy Stories 140

G

Gender Wars 146

Golf War...162

H

Hail to the Chief...212

Heaven's Gate...235

High Finance...242

Higher Education..245

Horizontal Tango..249

I

Indoor Sports 282

Information Systems....................................285

K

A Kick in the Balls....................................292

L

Legal Matters...296
Let There Be Light....................................298

M

Marital Bliss...304
Matters of Judgement 309
Medical Matters 312
Motoring Matters......................................327
Multiculturalism......................................328

N

Big Names...352

O

Onward Christian Soldiers.............................362
Old Age 389
Olympic Spirit 394
Oxymorons 396

P

Peacekeeping..400

Q

The Big Questions 404
Q&A 409

R

Random Thoughts....................................420
Recipes for Disaster.................................423
Rural Sector...427

S

Scientific Inquiry.....................................432
Self-help 435
Shop Till You Drop 438
Sports Report...445

T

Thespian Tendencies................................452
The Truth, the Whole Truth &
Nothing but the Truth 453

W

Why Did the Chicken Cross the Road?......................456

Words of Wisdom.......................................462

Index...469

INTRODUCTION

Ever since the invasion of this continent by the Brits, intent on transforming the place into a gulag for George III, we've worried about further invasions. Forever scanning the horizon. Perhaps it's a symptom of collective guilt.

Now, as Australia prepares for a D-Day-scale invasion of athletes, officials, tourists and the pestilential media, let us recall some of our historical anxieties.

First and foremost, the white colonists who'd grabbed the best real estate were panic merchants about Asian immigration. Given that maps put North at the top and South at the bottom, we saw the Yellow Peril as a gravitational imperative. Billions of Chinese would filter down through South-East Asia to fill our vast continent, like grains of yellow sand finding the accommodating emptiness of an hourglass. Hence the decision, at Federation, to have a White Australia Policy.

At about the same time cries of 'The Russians are coming!' could be heard from cliff and headland as the odd battleship *Potemkin*, sent on a goodwill tour by the tsar, was utterly misunderstood. To this day massive constructions, designed to accommodate cannon that would keep the Romanovs at bay, can be discovered decaying around our coastline.

After an historic run-in with the Japanese, who were truly planning to invade, we opted for Cold War paranoia and lived in dread of the domino theory as, one by one, our neighbours would be bolshevised until, at last, we'd wake up one morning living in an Australian soviet. This is the principal reason we saddled up for both the Korean and Vietnam wars.

And after the latter conflict, we became alarmed by 'boat people', refugees fleeing the communist victory – closely followed by Cambodians seeking to escape from Pol Pot.

While the numbers were modest, the anxieties were extreme. The White Australia Policy was officially dead, but the malady lingered on.

More recently, the panic merchants have tried to frighten Australians with two separate invasions –

of a new generation of boat people on the one hand, and American marching bands on the other. The high-stepping trumpeters were to have played a major part in the opening ceremonies of the Olympic Games but local shock-jocks aroused their listeners' xenophobia and the invitations were notoriously and expensively cancelled.

Which left the other threat. A few boatloads of poor wretches fleeing the tyrannies of the Taliban, Teheran and the tender mercies of Saddam Hussein.

Given that the entire non-Aboriginal population of Australia were boat people themselves, or descendants thereof, you'd think we'd have learnt some common sense. Or compassion. Aborigines must be very amused by our outbursts of bigotry for, for them, the worst boat people of all were the first – the sailors in the *Endeavour*, under Captain Cook's command, a clear case of 'there goes the neighbourhood'.

Mind you, Australia's attitude to invasion has been intensified by our experiences with the non-human. Rabbits are the classic case. A few pair were imported for pot-shotting on a country property at

Werribee, in Victoria, and within a few years, the entire nation had wall-to-wall carpeting. And think of the cane toads, imported to munch on the bugs that were munching the sugar cane. Here's a classic case of the cure being worse than the disease. Now it's only a matter of time until marching armies of toads push the human population into the sea. And we've been similarly threatened by various invasions of vegetation, like the all-engulfing prickly pear.

What do these invasions have to do with jokes? Well, while we preoccupy ourselves with the afore-mentioned panics, the most successful of all invasions has been taking place for the last 100 years. And we've welcomed it with open arms. American popular culture gained a toehold in Australia after the US Civil War when freed slaves, seeking employment, formed their own minstrel shows in America to compete with the huge and hugely successful productions mounted by white people parodying the Africans. Far from being welcomed to share the market, the white companies ran the newly formed black companies out of town and quite a few sought asylum in Australia where they played Melbourne,

Sydney and the goldfields. Overnight, the British music hall began to lose its tenure as audiences flocked to the more energetic, more exuberant African-Americans. So in the late 19th century, Australians started singing Stephen Foster medleys and we've been singing America's songs ever since.

Ditto for our cinema. Although we could lay claim to having produced the world's first feature films, although we were getting a head of steam up in local production (Australia turned out hundreds of features in the silent era), our industry was taken over and crushed by the might of Hollywood. (It took 40 years before we rejigged their feature industry, but even after massive amounts of government funding and considerable success at international film festivals, around $93 out of every $100 spent at the local box office is for an American film, leaving $6 or $7 for Australia to share with the rest of the world. The films of the UK, France, Italy, Germany etc. have to share, with us, the crumbs from the rich man's table.)

This pattern has been largely repeated in television where, apart from the market share of

Australian soaps, the programming (and particularly the programming on pay channels) is as American as anything you'd be likely to see in Manhattan or Memphis.

The invasion of American culture is virtually complete. We have dragged hundreds of Trojan Horses into our cinemas, our bookshops and our lounge rooms. We have clapped and cheered and thrown our money at the invading armies. Insofar as their impact on Australia, MGM is more influential than the CIA, while Paramount is more powerful than the Pentagon. Though soldiers are replaced by entertainers we are an occupied society as, across the board, American energies overwhelm Australian idioms.

And nowhere is this more obvious than with jokes.

When we started collecting Australian jokes about ten years ago we found hundreds that seemed authentically Australian, as antipodean as the euca-lypt, as culturally specific as kangaroo or koala.

But, progressively, we became aware of problems. First of all, the apparently pure, perfect, pristine

Australian joke turned out to be fully imported.

Take the joke told to us by Bob Hawke, then Australia's Prime Minister: 'There are two corpses on the Hume Highway. One's a dead politician, the other's a dead wombat. What's the difference? Answer: There are skid marks before the wombat.'

This seemed redolent with Australia's irreverent, anti-hierarchical attitude to its elites, if politicians could be thus classified. Imagine our astonishment, and disappointment, when we learnt that the Prime Minister's joke had originally been located on Route 66, where the corpses belonged to a politician and a skunk. (And, of course, the joke works even better with a skunk.)

Then there are jokes *about* prime ministers. We collected a number attacking Bob Hawke's successor, Paul Keating, only to discover that they'd originated in Munich in the 1930s when the target was Adolf Hitler. Furthermore, they were created by a couple of professional comics who ended up in Dachau.

We reconciled ourselves to the obvious truth. That the Australian joke was becoming an oxymoron. That the jokes that bounced around the landscape

like Australia's marsupials were of foreign manu-
facture. That all we did was provide them with different costumes, set them in a different landscape and
tell them in a different accent.

What increasingly concerned us was the obvious
fact that, overwhelmingly, the jokes Australians told,
like the films Australians watched and the songs
Australians listened to on radio or CD, whether
from Broadway shows or rap bands, were as American as Coca-Cola or the Big Mac (and there are
two more examples of the US invasion). Now this
process is accelerating at the speed of light with the
invasion of the Internet. Here's a technology that has
American jokes, invented in response to a Clintonian
embarrassment or a Kennedy plane crash, being told
in Australian pubs and taxis the next morning.

Within the last five years we've observed the
few remaining Australian colloquialisms being oblit-
erated by American counterparts. (For example, that
fine word 'drongo' has effectively been replaced by
'dickhead'.) Australian jokes, even hybridised jokes
that localise an American original, are disappearing.
Rather like rabbits overwhelmed by the calicivirus.

Now we don't bother hybridising them. We tell American jokes, raw and in the original.

This being the case, your editors suspect that this will be the last of our collections of Australian jokes because, quite frankly, there aren't any. Not any more. They are at very least an endangered species and may well prove to be extinct. Of course, any readers who glimpse an Australian joke through the foliage, like those fugitive sightings of the Tasmanian tiger, should contact the authorities. Which, in this case, is us.

Let it be said that the jokes in this book are, almost without exception, as 'introduced' as the rabbit or cane toad. Here is further evidence of the most comprehensive and complete takeover of one culture by another in the annals of human history.

Long besieged by US culture, Australia is now entirely in its thrall and consequently we include, without apology, quite a number of characteristic Clinton–Lewinsky jokes as evidence of this process of osmosis.

Clearly, Australians would have preferred to hybridise the jokes. Had we had a prime minister who was having oral sex with a female staffer this undoubtedly would have happened. But, thus far, no such scandal has surfaced. Or if it has occurred, other people are keeping their mouths shut. So while we await a whistleblower, if you'll forgive the expression, we'll laugh at Monica and Bill. For Australians are as well informed on Washington mores as anyone in the belt-way.

Australia, host to the Olympics. Australia, celebrating the centenary of its federation. Australia, one of the oldest democracies on earth. Australia, vast of acreage and rich of asset. This Australia is being nibbled away from the edges, by the globalisation of commerce and culture. And make no mistake – for Australians, globalisation is another word for Americanisation. Once we were invaded by rabbits. These days, it's by Barbie dolls.

But at least America's jokes make this process of cultural capitulation less painful. They allow Australians to laugh while their culture, such as it is, such as it was, goes down the gurgler.

A

ANZAC SPIRIT

AUSTRALIAN LIMERICKS

AVIATION

AZARIA

ANZAC SPIRIT

Two New Zealanders board a Qantas flight in London. Just before take-off an Australian bloke gets on and takes the aisle seat beside them. He kicks off his shoes, wiggles his toes and is just settling down for a kip when the Kiwi in the window seat says: 'I think I'll get a Coke.'

'No trubs,' says the Aussie, 'I'll get it for you.'

While he's gone the Kiwi picks up one of the Aussie's shoes and spits in it. When he returns with the Coke, the other Kiwi says: 'Could I have one too?'

The Australian kindly goes to fetch it and while he's away the other Kiwi picks up the other shoe and spits in it. The Aussie returns with the Coke and they all sit back to enjoy the flight.

As the plane is landing, the Australian slips his feet into his shoes and immediately knows what has happened.

'How long must this go on?' the Aussie asks. 'The hatred between our people ... the animosity ... the rivalry ... the spitting in shoes and the pissing in Cokes?'

* * *

An Australian ventriloquist was on holiday in New Zealand. While strolling through a small town in the South Island he saw an old bloke sitting at the side of the road patting his dog. Behind him was his horse and a sheep.

'G'day mate,' said the ventriloquist. 'That's a great-looking dog. Mind if I have a chat with him?'

The New Zealander says: 'The dog doesn't talk, ya stupid Aussie.'

The ventriloquist ignored him. 'Hey dog, how's it going?'

The dog replied: 'Doing all right.'

The New Zealander was astonished.

The ventriloquist continued: 'Is this Kiwi your owner?'

'Yep,' said the dog.

'How does he treat you?'

'Real good,' the dog seemed to say. 'He gives me good tucker and takes me for two walks a day.'

The ventriloquist then asked the New Zealander if he could talk to his horse.

The New Zealander said, rather defiantly, 'The horse doesn't talk.'

'G'day horse. How's it going?'

'Fine, fine,' said the horse.

'How does your owner treat you?'

'Pretty good, thanks for asking. He rides me regularly, brushes me down often and keeps me in the shed to protect me from the cold weather.'

By now the New Zealander was absolutely astonished.

'Mind if I talk to your sheep?' said the ventriloquist.

The New Zealander replied: 'The sheep's a bloody liar!'

Why do New Zealanders like to screw sheep on the edge of cliffs?
Because they push back so nicely.

AUSTRALIAN LIMERICKS

A robotic brothel in Hay
Uses EFTPOS to let clients pay
When you're right to go in
Select account type and PIN
When you're ready to come, press OK.

* * *

A footy supporter from Sydney
Had trouble controlling his kidney
To avoid the urinal
Throughout the Grand Final
He pissed in his pocket now, didn' he?

* * *

Before Sydney 2000 succumbs
To chinless Charles and his chums
Sack all remnant Royals
Those irrelevant boils
On emerging Republican bums.

* * *

Should Australian science espouse
Split genes and the transgenic mouse
Making test tubes grow wool
Putting tits on a bull
And pricks in Parliament House?

AVIATION

Air traffic control: 'Flight 1234, for noise abatement, turn right 45 degrees.'

Pilot: 'Roger, but we're at 35 000 feet. How much noise can we make up here?'

Air traffic control: 'Have you ever heard the noise a 747 makes when it hits an airbus?'

AZARIA

Some geologists are peering at rocks 100 km north of Uluru in the hope of finding fossilised crustacea, when they spot a naked teenager running with a pack of dingoes. Bouncing after her in the Land-cruiser, they manage to lasso her and, braving the snarls of the dingoes, toss her onto the back seat. She looks at them with wide, wild eyes while emitting doglike noises.

No sooner have they arrived at Alice Springs with the feral girl than the word goes out, all over Australia, all over the world, that 'they've found Azaria!' And DNA tests confirm that, yes, it is Azaria Chamberlain. What's more, the young woman shows every sign of shrewd intelligence. She is returned to her mother and, with Lindy's tutelage, quickly learns the English language and shows a remarkable aptitude for the higher realms of mathematics. But most of all she adores quantum mechanics.

Admitted to the University of Sydney she completes a four-year course within six months. The academic community is agog. Here is a girl reared by dogs in the desert who shows every sign of scientific genius. She appears on the ABC's *Australian Story* and subsequently on *60 Minutes* (both the local and US editions) and is a cover girl for every imaginable journal and magazine. She graduates with first-class honours in every subject.

But the very next day she's run over by a bus while chasing a car.

BABES & SUCKLINGS

BARS, BEER & BLOKES

BLONDE BOMBSHELLS

BUMPER STICKERS

BUSINESS ADVICE

BABES & SUCKLINGS

Thinking of having kids? Follow these lessons before you book the obstetrician:

Lesson One

1 Pick up the paper.
2 Read it for the last time.

Lesson Two

1 Between the hours of 5 p.m. and 10 p.m., tune a radio to loud static and walk around the lounge room carrying a wet bag weighing approximately 6 kg.
2 Put the bag down, set the alarm for midnight and go to sleep.
3 Between 12 and 1 a.m. get up and walk around the lounge room again, with the bag.
4 Set the alarm for 3 a.m.

5 2 a.m.: Get up and make a drink so you can get back to sleep.

6 2.45 a.m.: Go back to bed.

7 3 a.m.: Get up, the alarm went off.

8 Sing songs in the dark until 4 a.m. Again, with the wet bag.

9 Set the alarm for 5 a.m.

10 Get up. Make breakfast. Keep this up for five years. Look cheerful.

Lesson Three

1 Smear peanut butter onto the couch and jam onto the curtains.

2 Stick your fingers in poo.

3 Rub them on clean walls.

4 Cover the stains with crayon.

Lesson Four

1 Buy an octopus and a small bag made of loose mesh.

2 Attempt to put the octopus into the bag so that none of the arms hang out.

Lesson Five

1 Take an egg carton. Using a pair of scissors and a pot of paint, turn it into a crocodile.

2 Now take the tube from a roll of toilet paper. Using only Scotch tape and a piece of foil, turn it into an attractive Christmas candle.

3 Take a milk carton, a ping-pong ball and an empty Coco Pops packet. Make an exact replica of the Eiffel Tower.

Lesson Six

1 Buy a chocolate ice-cream cone and put it in the glove box of your car. Leave it there.

2 Get a dollar coin. Stick it in the cassette player.

3 Take a family-size packet of chocolate biscuits. Mash them into the back seat.

4 Run a garden rake along both sides of the car. There. Perfect.

Lesson Seven

1 Make a recording of Fran Drescher saying 'Mummy' repeatedly.

2 Leave no more than a four-second delay between each 'Mummy'.

3 Include an occasional crescendo of this sound to the decibel level of a supersonic jet.

4 Play this tape in your car everywhere you go for the next four years.

Lesson Eight

1 Borrow a pitbull terrier.

2 Borrow a child safety seat and put it in the back seat of your car.

3 Put the pitbull terrier in the seat.

Okay, now you're ready.

Little Teddy was walking down the hall when he heard a strange noise coming from his parents' bedroom. 'Dad! Dad! What are you doing?'

His father replied: 'I'm playing cards.'

The boy asked: 'Who's your partner?'

And Dad replied: 'Your mother.'

A couple of days later Dad was walking down the hall and heard a strange noise from the child's room. And he called: 'Teddy! What are you doing?'

Teddy replied: 'I'm playing cards.'

'And who's your partner?'

'With a hand this good,' said the boy, 'you don't need a partner!'

*　　*　　*

A little boy asked his father the difference between reality and theory. 'Son, go and ask your mother if she would sleep with another man for $1 million.'

So the boy asked his mother. 'Well, son, your father and I have been through a lot over the years and I really love him. But $1 million would set us up for retirement so I would have to say yes. Yes, I would.'

The boy asked his newly engaged sister the same question. 'Well, little brother, I love my fiancé a lot but we have to raise the deposit on a house and it'd be good to go to Fiji on our honeymoon. So, yes, I would.'

The boy repeated the responses to his father who told him: 'Okay, in theory we're sitting on $2 million. In reality, we're living with a couple of sluts.'

A little boy came home from school with numerous scratches. And his clothes were torn to shreds. His mother, horrified at his appearance, said: 'Oh, Billy, Billy, how often have I told you not to play with that naughty Smith boy?'

But he regarded his mother with an expression of deep disgust. 'Do I look as if I've been playing with anybody?'

Teacher: 'In which of his battles was King Gustav Adolphus of Sweden slain?'

Student: 'I'm pretty sure it was his last one.'

While pregnant with triplets, a woman was the victim of a drive-by shooting. It was an entirely random incident but when she awoke in hospital they told her that she'd been shot three times. 'Fortunately no serious harm seems to have been done to you or the babies. But we're reluctant to remove the bullets for fear of triggering a crisis.'

Every day the woman grew stronger and stronger, and in due course, she had the three babies – two beautiful little girls and a strong little boy.

The mother had completely forgotten about the bullets until a few years later, when her first daughter came running into the kitchen shouting: 'Mummy, come and look at this!' She pointed into the toilet bowl and there was a bullet. A few weeks later her other daughter came rushing in: 'Mummy, Mummy, come and look in the toilet!' And, yes, she'd shat the second bullet.

A few more years passed. Then the little boy came rushing in and said: 'Mummy, Mummy, I was having a fart and shot the dog!'

The phone rings and a little boy answers it.

The caller says: 'Is your mummy there?'

In a whisper, the little boy replies: 'Yes.'

'Can I speak with her?'

'She's busy.'

'Is your daddy there?'

'Yes.'

'Can I speak with him?'

'He's busy.'

'Is there anyone else there?'

'The fire brigade.'

'Well, can I talk to one of them?'

'They're busy.'

'Is there anyone else there?'

'The police are here.'

'Well, can I talk to one of them?'

'They're busy.'

'Let me get this straight. Your mother, your father, the fire brigade and the police are all at your house. And they're all busy. What are they doing?'

'They're looking for me.'

A boy was told by a classmate that most adults are hiding at least one dark secret, and that this makes it very easy to blackmail them by saying: 'I know the whole truth.' The boy decides to go home and try it out. He goes home, and as he is greeted by his mother, he says: 'I know the whole truth.' His mother quickly hands him $20 and says: 'Just don't tell your father.'

Quite pleased, the boy waits for his father to get home from work and greets him with: 'I know the whole truth.' The father promptly hands him $40 and says: 'Please don't say a word to your mother.'

Very pleased, the boy is on his way to school the next day when he sees the postman at his front door. The boy greets him by saying: 'I know the whole truth.' The postman drops the mail, opens his arms, and says: 'Then come and give your father a big hug!'

On Jimmy's first day of first grade, he raised his hand as soon as the teacher came into the room and said: 'I don't belong here, I should be in the third grade!'

The teacher looked at little Jimmy's records and told him to please take his seat. Not five minutes passed before little Jimmy stood up again and said: 'I don't belong here, I should be in the third grade!'

Jimmy did this a few more times before the principal came along and the teacher explained Jimmy's problem. The principal and the first-grade teacher told little Jimmy that if he could answer some questions they could decide in which grade he belonged. Well, they soon discovered that Jimmy knew all the state capitals and country capitals that the principal could think of. The teacher suggested they try some biology questions. 'What does a cow have four of but a woman only two?' asked the teacher.

'Legs,' Jimmy immediately replied.

'What does a man have in his pants that a woman doesn't?' asked the teacher.

'Pockets!' said Jimmy.

The teacher looked at the principal, who said: 'Maybe he should be in third grade. I missed those last two questions!'

*   *   *

A little girl runs out into the backyard where her father is working, and asks him: 'Daddy, what's sex?'

'Okay,' he thinks, 'this day was bound to come, and I'm not going to let my little princess learn about sex from the streets.' So he sits her down and tells her all about the birds and the bees. He tells her about conception, sexual intercourse, sperm and eggs. He tells her about puberty, menstruation, erections, wet dreams.

Then she asks: 'Daddy, what's a couple?'

And he carries on: a couple are the two people involved in the sex, but this can be two males also, where they penetrate from the arse, or two females which they call lesbians, where they use the tongue on the vagina ... and goes on to describe mastur-

bation, oral sex, group sex, pornography, bondage
and rape, paedophilia, sex toys etc . . .

The father finally asks: 'So why did you want
to know about a couple?'

'Oh, Mummy said lunch would be ready in a
couple of secs . . .'

☆   ☆   ☆

A young boy is in his room playing with himself
when his mother comes in and catches him.

'If you keep doing that you'll go blind!' she
yells.

The boy replies: 'Well, can I keep doing it until
I need glasses?'

BARS, BEER &
BLOKES

An angry wife met her husband at the door. There was alcohol on his breath and lipstick on his collar. 'I assume,' she snarled, 'that there is a very good reason for you to come waltzing in here at six o'clock in the morning?'

'There is,' he replied. 'Breakfast.'

* * *

A baby seal walks into a bar and the bartender says: 'What'll ya have?'

The seal says: 'Anything but a Canadian Club!'

* * *

A termite walks into a bar and says: 'Is the bar tender here?'

✲　✲　✲

Late one Friday night a policeman spotted a man driving very erratically through the streets of Dublin. He pulled him over and asked if he had been drinking that evening.

'Aye, so I have. 'Tis Friday, you know, so me and the lads stopped by the pub where I had six or seven pints. And then there was something called "Happy Hour" and they served these mar-gar-itos which are quite good. So I had four or five o' those. Then I had to drive me friend Mike home and o' course I had to go in for a couple of Guinness – couldn't be rude, ye know. Then I stopped on the way home to get another bottle for later.' And the man fumbled around in his coat until he located his bottle of whisky, which he held up for inspection.

The officer sighed and said: 'Sir, I'm afraid I'll need you to step out of the car and take a breathalyser test.'

Indignantly, the man said; 'Why? Don't ye believe me???!!'

A bloke walks into a pub one night. He goes up to the bar and asks for a beer.

'Certainly, sir, that'll be one cent.'

'One cent?' exclaims the bloke.

The barman says, 'Yes.'

So the bloke glances over at the menu and asks, 'Could I have a nice juicy T-bone steak, with chips, peas and a fried egg?'

'Certainly sir,' replies the bartender, 'but that all comes to real money.'

'How much money?' inquires the bloke.

'Four cents,' he replies.

'*Four* cents!' exclaims the bloke. 'Where's the bloke who owns this place?'

The barman replies: 'Upstairs with my wife.'

The bloke says, 'What's he doing with your wife?'

The bartender replies, 'The same as I'm doing with his business.'

A bloke walks into a pub and notices he's the only one there, apart from the bartender, who's on the phone. The bartender signals him that he'll be with him in a minute. The bloke nods and waits at the bar.

Suddenly he hears a little voice say: 'Hey, you're looking pretty sharp today. New suit?'

The bloke looks around but can't see anyone else in the place. He hears the voice again. 'Seriously ... you are looking good, mate. Have you lost weight?'

The bloke looks around again, and still doesn't see anyone. 'Hello?' he asks. 'Is someone speaking to me?'

'You bet! I just had to say that I thought you were looking great!' Other tiny voices suddenly rose in agreement. The bloke realises now that these voices are coming from a bowl of beer nuts on the bar in front of him. He stares at them as the bartender finally hangs up and comes to serve his only customer.

'What will you have?' he asks.

'Oh, a glass of beer, I guess,' mutters the bloke, still staring at the nuts.

He finally looks up at the bartender pouring his beer. 'What's the deal with these nuts?' he asks.

The bartender brings the beer over, sets it before him and says: 'They're complimentary!'

A bloke is about to walk into a nightclub when a bouncer tells him that it's compulsory to wear a tie, otherwise no admission. So the bloke returns to his car and searches unsuccessfully for a tie. Then he remembers that he's got a set of jumper leads in the boot and, in desperation, ties them around his neck. He goes back to the nightclub and the bouncer looks him over, and says: 'Well, okay, I suppose it's all right to let you in. Just don't start anything.'

A bloke sat in a pub, just drinking a beer and minding his own business, when all of a sudden, a big hoon came in, knocked him off his stool and said: 'That was a karate chop from Korea!'

The bloke dusted himself down, got back on the stool and had another beer. All of a sudden the hoon knocked him down again and said: 'That was a judo chop from Japan!'

He'd had enough of this treatment and left the pub, only to return 15 minutes later and, with a huge WHACK!, knocked the hoon unconscious.

And he looked at the barman, and said: 'When he wakes up, tell him that's a crowbar from Mitre 10.'

Two men were adrift in a lifeboat following a dramatic escape from a sinking ship. While rummaging through the boat's provisions, one of the men stumbled across an old lamp. Secretly hoping that a genie would appear, he rubbed the lamp vigorously. To the amazement of the castaways, one did come forth.

This particular genie, however, stated that she could only deliver one wish, not the standard three.

Without giving much thought to the matter, the man blurted out: 'Make the entire ocean into beer!'

Immediately the genie clapped her hands with a deafening crash, and the entire sea turned into the finest brew ever sampled by mortals.

Simultaneously, the genie vanished to her freedom.

Only the gentle lapping of beer on the hull broke the stillness as the men considered their circumstances.

The other man looked disgustedly at the one whose wish had been granted. After a long, tension-filled moment, he spoke.

'Nice going! Now we're going to have to pee in the boat!'

☆　☆　☆

A bloke walks into a pub with his pet monkey. He orders a drink and while he's drinking it, the monkey jumps around all over the place. The monkey grabs some olives off the bar and eats them, then grabs some limes and eats them. He then jumps onto the pool table, grabs the cue ball, sticks it in his mouth and swallows it whole.

The barman screams at the bloke: 'Did you see what your monkey just did?'

'No, what?' says the bloke.

'He just ate the cue ball off my pool table, whole!' says the barman.

'Yeah, that doesn't surprise me,' replies the patron. 'He eats everything in sight, the little jerk. I'll pay for the cue ball.' He finishes his drink, pays the bill and leaves the pub.

Two weeks later, he's in the pub again and has his monkey with him. He orders a drink and the monkey starts running around. While the man is finishing his drink, the monkey finds a maraschino cherry on the bar. He grabs it, sticks it up his arse, pulls it out and eats it.

The barman is disgusted. 'Did you see what your monkey did now?' he asks.

'What?' inquires the patron.

'Well, he stuck a maraschino cherry up his arse, then pulled it out and ate it,' says the barman.

'Yeah, that doesn't surprise me,' replies the bloke. 'He still eats everything in sight, but ever since he swallowed that cue ball, he measures everything first.'

A drunk walks into a crowded pub and takes the last barstool, next to an older woman. After a while, the woman starts to smell a horrible odour coming from the direction of the drunk. She turns to him and says: 'Excuse me, Mister, but did you just shit yourself?'

The drunk replies: 'Yes ma'am, I have indeed shit myself.'

The woman says: 'Well, why don't you go somewhere and clean yourself up?'

The drunk says: 'Cos I'm not finished yet ...'

McQuillan walked into a bar and ordered martini after martini, each time removing the olives and placing them in a jar. When the jar was filled with olives and all the drinks consumed, the Irishman started to leave.

'S'cuse me,' said a customer, who was puzzled over what McQuillan had done. 'What was that all about?'

'Nothing,' said the Irishman. 'My wife just sent me out for a jar of olives.'

* * *

Three vampires walk into a bar. The waitress comes up to them and asks them what they'll have. The first vampire says: 'I'll have a glass of O Positive.'

The second vampire says: 'I'll have a glass of AB Negative.'

The third vampire says: 'It's my turn to drive. So I'll just have a glass of plasma.'

The waitress turns towards the barman and yells: 'Give me two bloods and one blood lite!'

* * *

The Lone Ranger and Tonto walked into a bar one day and sat down to drink a beer. After a few minutes, a big tall cowboy walked in and said: 'Who owns the white horse outside?'

The Lone Ranger stood up, hitched his gun belt, and said: 'I do. Why?'

The cowboy looked at the Lone Ranger and said: 'I just thought you would like to know that your horse is just about dead!' The Lone Ranger and Tonto rushed outside and, sure enough, Silver was about dead from heat exhaustion. The Lone Ranger got him some water and made him drink it, and soon Silver was starting to feel a little better.

The Lone Ranger turned to Tonto and said: 'Tonto, I want you to run around Silver and see if you can create enough of a breeze to make him feel better.'

So Tonto took off running in circles around Silver. Not able to do anything else but wait, the Lone Ranger returned to the bar to finish his drink.

A few minutes later, another cowboy struts to the bar and announces: 'Who owns that big white horse outside?'

The Lone Ranger stands again and claims: 'I do. What's wrong with him this time?'

The cowboy says to him: 'Nothing much. I just wanted you to know that you left your Injun running!'

* * *

A bloke walks into a pub and orders a double whisky. The barman can't help but notice that the bloke seems very, very depressed.

'What's wrong?'

'I got home and found my wife having sex with my best friend.'

'Oh, you poor bastard,' says the barman. 'Have another one on me.'

As the bloke downs his second drink, the barman asks: 'And what did you do?'

'I walked over to my wife,' the man replies, 'looked her straight in the eye and told her that we were through. I told her to pack her stuff and bugger off.'

'And what about your friend?'

'I walked over to him, looked him straight in the eye and said "BAD DOG!".'

* * *

A duck walks into a pub and asks: 'Got any peanuts?'

The barman says no.

The duck walks out.

The duck walks in the next day and asks: 'Got any peanuts?'

The barman says no.

The duck walks out.

The duck walks in the next day and asks: 'Got any peanuts?'

The barman says: 'I told you yesterday and the day before that I haven't got any bloody peanuts! If you ask one more time, I'll nail your beak shut!'

The duck walks out.

The duck comes back the next day and asks: 'Got any nails?'

The barman says no.

The duck says: 'Good. Got any peanuts?'

* * *

A drunk is pissing into a fountain in the middle of a shopping mall. A policeman comes up to him and says: 'Stop that! And put it away!'

The drunk puts his penis back into his pants and zips up. As the policeman turns to go, the drunk starts laughing.

'What's so funny?'

'I fooled you,' says the drunk. 'I put it away. But I didn't stop!'

* * *

A drunken bloke staggers into a Catholic church and sits down in a confessional box and says nothing. The bewildered priest coughs to attract his attention. But still the man says nothing. The priest then knocks on the wall three times in a final attempt to get the man to speak.

Finally, the drunk replies: 'No use knockin' mate, there's no paper in this one either.'

* * *

Two drunks are sitting at the bar staring into their drinks. 'Hey, cobber, you ever seen an ice cube with a hole in it before?'

'Yes. I've been married to one for 15 years.'

* * *

Two blokes are walking their dogs. One's a Doberman and the other's a chihuahua. They pass a restaurant and decide to get something to eat.

The bloke with the chihuahua says: 'We can't go in there. We've got dogs with us. And there's a sign saying "No Dogs Allowed".'

And the bloke with the Doberman says: 'Just follow my example.'

He puts on a pair of dark glasses and walks through the restaurant door with his Doberman.

'Sorry sir, no pets allowed,' says the waitress.

'But you don't understand. This is my seeing-eye dog.'

The waitress says: 'A Doberman? I thought they were usually Labradors.'

'Yes, they're using Dobermans now. They're very good.'

'I'm sorry, sir. Of course you can come in,' says the waitress.

Then the bloke with the chihuahua follows suit. He puts on a pair of dark glasses and starts to walk in.

Once again the waitress says: 'Sorry sir, no pets allowed.'

And the bloke with the chihuahua says: 'But you don't understand. This is my seeing-eye dog.'

And the waitress says: 'A chihuahua?'

And the man with the chihuahua says: 'A chihuahua?? They gave me a chihuahua?!'

✱   ✱   ✱

A bloke went to the pub for a drink after work and couldn't help noticing a man in the far corner passed out over his beer. He was very drunk and incoherent. Deciding to do his good deed for the day, the bloke checked the man's wallet and found his address. Then he tried to help the man stand up. But he kept falling down. Dragging him heaving, the bloke finally carried the drunk outside and got him into his car. When he reached the drunk's house he pulled him out of the car but he still couldn't stand up. So the bloke sought help from passers-by, dragged the bloke to the front door and rang the bell. It was opened by a woman and he explained that he'd brought her husband home. 'Thank you very much,' she said. 'But where did you leave his wheelchair?'

✫   ✫   ✫

A bloke walked into a pub and said to the barman: 'I'll have a glass of beer. But not too hot. And not too cold. But right in the groove.'

The next day he came back and asked the barman for a glass of beer. 'Not too hot. Not too cold. But right in the groove.'

To which the barman responded: 'Why don't you kiss my arse! Not on the left cheek. Not on the right cheek. But right in the groove!'

* * *

A bear walks into a bar and sits down. He bangs on the bar with his paw and demands a beer. The barman approaches and says: 'We don't serve beer to bears in bars in Billings, Montana.'

The bear, becoming angry, again demands a beer. The barman again tells him: 'We don't serve beer to bears in bars in Billings, Montana.'

The bear, very angry now, says: 'If you don't serve me a beer I'm going to eat that lady sitting at the end of the bar.'

The barman once again says: 'Sorry, but we don't serve beer to bears in bars in Billings, Montana.'

So the bear goes to the end of the bar and eats the woman. He returns to his bar stool and says: 'Give me a beer.'

And, yet again, the barman says: 'Sorry, we don't serve beer to bears in bars in Billings, Montana, particularly if they're on drugs.'

The bear says: 'I'm not on drugs.'

The barman says: 'Yes you are! That was a barbitchyouate.'

*   *   *

A barman was very proud of the fact that he could squeeze a lemon so that no more juice would come out of it. He made a standing offer of $1000 to anyone who could get more juice out of a lemon after he'd squeezed it. Every night big, burly regulars at the bar attempted to get more juice from a lemon he'd squeezed, but no one could produce so much as a drop. But one night a little bloke walked in and said he'd heard of the standing offer and would like to try. The barman said: 'How do you think you could succeed when all these big blokes have failed?' And the little guy said: 'Just give me a chance and I'll show you.'

So the barman, thinking his regulars would enjoy the joke, picked up a lemon and squeezed it. After squeezing all the juice he could out of it he handed the dried rind to the little bloke and said: 'Here you go.' The little bloke took the lemon and squeezed it and managed to get one, two, three, four, five, *six* more drops of juice. Amazed, the barman said: 'Well, here's your $1000. But what do you do for a living? Are you a professional bodybuilder or what?' And the little bloke said: 'No, I work for the Tax Department.'

*　*　*

An Irishman walks into a pub in Dublin, orders three pints of Guinness and sits in the back of the room drinking a sip out of each one in turn. When he finishes them he comes back to the bar and orders three more. The barman says: 'You know, a pint goes flat after I draw it. Wouldn't it be better to buy one at a time?'

And the Irishman replies: 'Well, you see, I have two brothers. One lives in America, the other in Australia, and I'm here in Dublin. When we left home we promised that we'd drink this way, to remember the good old days when we could drink together.'

The barman is quite touched.

The Irishman becomes a regular in the pub, always drinking the same way. He orders three pints and drinks them in turn. But one day he comes in looking a bit sad and orders just two pints. The regulars notice and fall silent. When he comes back to the bar for the second round, the barman says: 'Look, I don't want to intrude on your grief, but I know we all want to offer condolences on your great loss.'

The Irishman looks puzzled for a moment. And then he laughs. 'Oh no,' he says, 'everyone's fine. I've decided to quit drinking.'

Practising at the Bar

Two offerings from the noticeboard of the Linga Longa pub, Gundy, New South Wales.

Prayer for Beer
Our lager
Which art in barrels
Hallowed be thy drink
Thy will be drunk
At home as it is in the pub

Give us this day our foamy head
And forgive us our spillages
As we forgive those who spill against us
And lead us not into incarceration
But deliver us from hangovers
For thine is the beer
The bitter, the lager
Barmen.

On a crudely hacked circle of cardboard:

This is a tuit. At long last we have a sufficient quantity for you to have one of your own. Guard it with your life! These tuits are hard to come by, especially the round ones! 'I'll do that as soon as I get a round tuit.' Now that you have a round tuit of your own, many things that you meant to do just may get done. So get tuit!

BLONDE BOMBSHELLS

A blonde's house catches on fire. So she calls the fire brigade. 'My house is on fire! My house is on fire!'

'How do we get there?' says the fire captain.

And she says: 'Duh! In the big red truck.'

* * *

A blonde goes to the doctor to lose weight and the doctor suggests that if she runs 8 km per day for 300 days she could lose a lot. So the blonde does this and calls the doctor after 300 days.

'Doctor, I lost the weight but there's a problem.'

'What's the problem?' asks the doctor.

'I'm 2400 km from home!'

* * *

A blonde is angry with the Tax Department and decides to blow it up. So she puts a bag of bombs in the back seat of her Celica and heads for Canberra. Her boyfriend is worried about her: 'What if the bombs blow up in the car?'

'Don't worry, darling,' she says, 'I've got a spare bomb in the boot.'

A blonde is standing at a vending machine putting money in the slot and collecting can after can after can of Coke. A bloke behind her is getting more and more impatient. 'For Christ's sake, hurry up!'

And she says: 'Can't you see I'm winning?'

How did the blonde get hurt raking leaves?
She fell out of the tree.

What do blondes say after sex?
Next!

What's the difference between a blonde and a mosquito?
A mosquito stops sucking when you slap it.

What's a blonde's idea of safe sex?
Locking the car door.

Why did the blonde cross the road?
Never mind. What was she doing out of the bedroom?

Why do blondes drive cars with sunroofs?
They've got more leg room.

☆　☆　☆

A blonde went to an auction sale and bought a Ming vase. She wanted it to go with her Ming coat.

☆　☆　☆

A blonde had a mum, a grandma and a great-grandma. She asked her mum: 'Mum, how much did you charge for a blow job in your day?' Her mum said: 'Twenty dollars, why?'

'Oh, just wondered.'

She asked her grandmother the same thing. She answered: 'Five pounds.'

Then she asked her great-grandma, who said: 'Well, because it was the war, we didn't charge anything as we were grateful for a warm drink.'

★　★　★

The scene is a Harvey Norman store. A blonde is asking a salesman: 'What kind of TV is this?'

He says: 'Sorry, we don't sell to blondes.'

She returns the next day, her hair dyed red, and asks a different salesman the same question.

'Sorry, we don't sell to blondes.'

She returns a week later having changed her whole appearance by putting on a false moustache and a goatee beard. And she disguises her voice by talking in a deep baritone. 'I want you to sell me that colour TV.'

'Sorry,' is the response, 'we don't sell to blondes.'

Whereupon she bursts into tears. 'Why, why, *why* won't you sell this TV to me?'

'Because it's a microwave.'

☆　☆　☆

A blonde, new to boating, was having a problem. No matter how hard she tried, she just couldn't get her brand new 7-metre powerboat to perform. It was sluggish in almost every manoeuvre no matter how much power she applied. After an hour of trying to get it going she put-putted over to a nearby marina. Perhaps they could tell her what was wrong.

A thorough topside check revealed everything was in perfect working order. The engine ran fine. The prop was the correct size and pitch.

So one of the blokes from the marina jumped into the water to check underneath the boat. He came up choking from laughing underwater. Under the boat, still strapped securely in place, was the trailer.

It's a long flight from Sydney to Perth, so the blonde settles down in her window seat with a cushion. She doesn't like the look of the bloke sitting beside her and is determined to get to sleep. But he wants to play games. 'Look, it's a really good game. We ask each other questions and if we're wrong it costs $5.' (As she's a blonde he's convinced he'll be able to win every time.)

'Sorry, but I really want to go to sleep.'

So he ups the ante. 'I'll tell you what, every time you're wrong you give me $5. And if I'm wrong, I give you $50.' She's still not interested.

'Okay, okay. If I'm wrong I'll give you $500!'

Now she's interested. The game begins. He asks her to name all the planets in our solar system. She hands him $5. And she asks him to answer a riddle. 'What goes upstairs with three legs, and comes down with four?'

He's puzzled. He can't think of the answer. He takes out his lap-top and using his high-tech modem searches the entire Internet for a possible answer. He connects with the National Library, with the Smithsonian in Washington. And he can't find the answer. With the plane halfway across the Nullarbor he wakes the blonde and hands her $500. She takes the money and turns back to sleep.

'Hang on! Hang on! What *is* the answer? What goes upstairs with three legs and comes down with four?'

Without a word, she hands him a $5 note.

☆ ☆ ☆

A blonde goes into David Jones and asks for a pair of alligator shoes. When she's told the price she's aghast. 'It would be cheaper for me to go out to the airport, buy a first-class ticket, fly to Los Angeles, change planes for Louisiana, buy a boat and a dirty great gun and kill my own alligator.'

And having said it, it sounds like a good idea. So she does. She catches a cab to Mascot, heads straight for the Louisiana swamps and starts wading waist-deep through the muddy waters, blazing away with her over-and-under. Passers-by see her shooting a 'gator coming straight for her and dragging it to the shore where it joins six other reptilian corpses.

And they hear her cursing: 'Fuck! Another one that isn't wearing shoes!'

✷ ✷ ✷

Why do blondes wash their hair in the kitchen sink?
That's where you clean vegetables.

Why did the blonde return her new scarf?
It was too tight.

What's a blonde's favourite nursery rhyme?
Humpme, Dumpme.

✷ ✷ ✷

A blonde climbs onto a Qantas flight at Tullamarine and tells the purser that she's flying first class to Sydney. 'I'm sorry, madam, but we don't have first class on domestic flights. Just business class.'

'All right,' says the woman, 'I'm flying business class to Sydney.'

63

'But you've only got an economy ticket.'

'That doesn't matter. I'm a remarkably beautiful blonde and I'm flying business class to Sydney.'

The purser refers the matter to the chief purser, who hears the same story. 'I am a gorgeous, beautiful, stunning blonde and I'm flying business class to Sydney.'

'But you've only got a coach ticket.'

'Doesn't matter. I'm a blonde and ...'

'Yes, yes, you're flying business class to Sydney. Just wait here a moment, madam, while I talk to the captain.'

The captain comes out to adjudicate.

'I'm a stunning, drop-dead-beautiful blonde and I'm flying business class to Sydney.'

The captain whispers something in her ear and her expression changes. She immediately walks to the other end of the plane and takes her economy seat.

'What did you tell her?' asks the purser.

'I told her that business class wasn't going to Sydney.'

✫   ✫   ✫

Why do brunettes like their dark hair colour?
It doesn't show the dirt.

Why are brunettes so proud of their hair?
It matches their moustache.

Why don't brunettes get breast implants?
They've already spent their money on thigh and
butt implants.

What did the frustrated brunette say to her
uninterested lover?
'What part of "yes" don't you understand?'

What do brunettes miss most about a great party?
The invitation.

Why do brunettes have to pay an extra $2000
for a breast job?
Because the plastic surgeon has to start from scratch.

How do you describe a brunette whose phone rings on Saturday night?
Startled.

What do you call a good-looking man with a brunette?
A hostage.

Who makes all the bras for brunettes?
Fisher-Price.

BUMPER STICKERS

If you smoke after sex, you're doing it too fast.

I don't suffer from insanity, I enjoy every minute of it.

If ignorance is bliss, you must be orgasmic.

Jesus is coming; everyone look busy.

WANTED: Meaningful overnight relationship.

So you're a feminist ... Isn't that cute!

Anyone can give up smoking, but it takes a real man to face cancer.

If: a two-letter word for futility.

Earth is the insane asylum for the universe.

To all you virgins, thanks for nothing.

I'm not a complete idiot; some parts are missing.

Earth first ... we'll mine the other planets later.

If something goes without saying, LET IT!

If at first you do succeed, try not to look astonished.

Work is for people who don't know how to fish.

Jesus loves you ... everyone else thinks you're an arsehole.

Jesus paid for our sins ... now let's get our money's worth.

Reality is a crutch for people who can't handle drugs.

Out of my mind. Back in five minutes.

Keep honking, I'm reloading.

Prevent inbreeding – ban country music.

Snatch a kiss, or vice versa.

I don't have to be dead to donate my organ.

Sometimes I wake up grumpy; other times I let her sleep.

I want to die in my sleep like my grandfather ... not screaming and yelling like the passengers in his car.

I said 'No' to drugs, but they just wouldn't listen.

So many recipes, so few cats.

I didn't fight my way to the top of the food chain to be a vegetarian.

Save a mouse ... eat a pussy!

It *is* as *bad* as you think, and they *are* out to get you.

Smile: it's the second-best thing you can do with your lips.

Wink. I'll do the rest!

If we aren't supposed to eat animals, why are they made of meat?

I know what you're thinking, and you should be ashamed of yourself.

Don't drink and drive: you might hit a bump and spill your drink.

We are born naked, wet and hungry. Then things get worse.

A dirty mind is a terrible thing to waste.

Lottery: a tax on people who are bad at maths.

Consciousness: that annoying time between naps.

Be nice to your kids. They'll choose your nursing home.

Ever stop to think, and forget to start again?

Sex on television can't hurt you unless you fall off.

Make it idiot-proof and someone will make a better idiot.

Diplomacy is the art of saying 'Nice doggie' till you can find a rock.

I'm a corporate executive; I keep things from happening.

Cover me – I'm changing lanes.

Change is inevitable, except from a vending machine.

I love cats ... they taste just like chicken.

Laugh alone and the world thinks you're an idiot.

The gene pool could use a little chlorine.

Don't blame me, I'm from Uranus.

When you do a good deed, get a receipt in case heaven is like the Tax Department.

I took an IQ test and the results were negative.

When there's a will, I want to be in it!

Okay, who stopped the payment of my reality check?

Time is the best teacher; unfortunately it kills all its students!

It's lonely at the top, but you eat better.

Warning: dates in the calendar are closer than they appear.

Give me ambiguity or give me something else.

He who laughs last thinks slowest.

Always remember you're unique, just like everyone else.

Friends help you move. Real friends help you move bodies.

Very funny, Scotty. Now beam down my clothes.

Wowserism: the haunting fear that someone, somewhere may be happy.

The sex was so good that even the neighbours had a cigarette.

Three kinds of people: those who can count and those who can't.

I like you, but I wouldn't want to see you working with subatomic particles.

I killed a six-pack just to watch it die.

BUSINESS ADVICE

It's a very expensive restaurant in Sydney and James Packer is lunching with Graham Richardson and John Laws. A young bloke comes over and asks Packer to forgive him for interrupting, 'but you've no idea how much I admire you – well, of course, all of you – but you, Mr Packer, are my hero. Now, I can't afford to come to a place like this normally but I'm trying to swing a business deal with someone who doesn't take me very seriously, who knows I'm not important, so I've saved up for months for this moment, in the hope of impressing him.'

Packer nods impatiently while Laws drums the tablecloth with his fingertips and Richardson stifles a yawn.

'So I'm here to ask you a favour. Something I've absolutely no right to do. But somehow I think you might just consider it. Because I feel you're that sort of person.'

'What is it?' snaps Packer.

'I was wondering if you could just wander over to my table at some point in the next hour or so and slap me on the back and say "G'day Arthur". Because that's my name, Arthur. It would impress the hell out of the bloke I'll be having lunch with and might well swing the deal for me. You know, just in passing. Slap me on the back and say "G'day Arthur".'

Packer grunts ambiguously and Laws tells Arthur to 'Bugger off, we're just trying to have a quiet lunch here, okay?'

So Arthur buggers off. And a few minutes later his client arrives.

From time to time Packer glances over and sees that things aren't going so well for Arthur. The client looks bored and deeply unimpressed.

So, what the hell! On his way to the toilet he does a detour, comes over to the table, gives Arthur a hearty slap on the back and says 'G'day Arthur! Forgive me for interrupting but it's great to see you again.'

And Arthur looks up and says: 'Bugger off, James. Can't you see I'm busy?'

✮   ✮   ✮

A man was dragged from his wrecked car with two small injuries. His ears. It was necessary for them to be amputated. While this had little effect on his hearing, he was immensely self-conscious about his appearance.

Prior to the accident he'd dreamt of having his own business. Using the insurance pay-out as capital he bought a small but profitable computer firm. But after a few weeks he realised that he lacked administrative skills and so decided to hire an office manager.

Three well-qualified candidates were short-listed and he interviewed each of them. The first interview went well. He found the young woman competent and likeable. His last question was: 'Do you notice anything unusual about me?' The woman said: 'Now that you mention it, you have no ears.' She didn't get the job.

The second interview was even more encouraging. This candidate, a university graduate, seemed particularly bright and had excellent references. Once again the final question was: 'Do you notice anything unusual about me?' 'Yes,' said the candidate, with a bright smile, 'you have no ears.' He didn't get the job either.

Fortunately the third candidate was even better than the other two. Convinced that he wanted to hire this applicant, the man once again asked: 'Do you notice anything unusual about me?' The applicant replied: 'Yeah. You're wearing contact lenses, aren't you?'

'That's very perceptive of you. How can you tell?'

'Well, you can't wear glasses when you don't have any fucking ears!'

Office work dull? None of your colleagues appreciate your humour? Amuse yourself. (Points are awarded on a degree-of-difficulty basis. You can award yourself extra points for creative execution.)

One-point Gags

1 Run one lap around the office at top speed.
2 Groan out loud in the toilet cubicle. (At least one other 'non-player' must be in the bathroom at the time.)
3 Ignore the first five people who say 'Good morning' to you.
4 Phone someone in the office you barely know, leave your name and say: 'Just called to say I can't talk right now. Bye.'
5 To signal the end of a conversation, clamp your hands over your ears and grimace.
6 When someone hands you a piece of paper, finger it, and whisper huskily, 'Mmmmmm, that feels soooo good!'
7 Leave your zipper open for one hour. If anyone points it out, say 'Sorry, I really prefer it that way.'

8 Walk sideways to the photocopier.

9 While riding in a lift, gasp dramatically every time the doors open.

Three-point Gags

1 Say to your boss 'I like your style,' and shoot him with double-barrelled fingers.

2 Babble incoherently at a fellow employee, then ask 'Did you get all that? I don't want to have to repeat it.'

3 Page yourself over the intercom (do not disguise your voice).

4 Kneel in front of the water cooler and drink directly from the nozzle. (There must be a 'non-player' within sight.)

5 Shout random numbers while someone is counting.

Five-point Gags

1 At the end of a meeting, suggest that, for once, it would be nice to conclude with the singing of the national anthem (extra points if you actually launch into it yourself).

2 Walk into a very busy person's office and while they watch you with growing irritation, turn the light switch on/off ten times.

3 For an hour, refer to everyone you speak to as 'Bob'.

4 Announce to everyone in a meeting that you 'really have to go and do number two'.

5 After every sentence, say 'mon' in a really bad Jamaican accent. As in 'The report's on your desk, mon.' Keep this up for one hour.

6 While an office mate is out, move their chair into the lift.

7 In a meeting or crowded situation, slap your forehead repeatedly and mutter 'Shut up, damn it, all of you just shut up!'

8 At lunchtime, get down on your knees and announce 'As God is my witness, I'll never go hungry again.'

9 In a colleague's diary, write: '10 a.m. See how I look in tights.'

10 Carry your keyboard over to your colleague and ask 'You wanna swap?'

11 Repeat the following conversation ten times to the same person: 'Do you hear that?' 'What?' 'Never mind. It's gone now.'

12 Come to work in army fatigues and when asked why, say 'I can't talk about it.'

13 Posing as a maître d', call a colleague and tell him he's won a lunch for four at a local restaurant. Let him go.

14 Speak with an accent (French, German, Porky Pig etc.) during a very important conference call.

15 Find the vacuum and start vacuuming around your desk.

16 Hang a two-foot long piece of toilet roll from the back of your pants and act genuinely surprised when someone points it out.

☆   ☆   ☆

Advice to the Boss on How to Enhance Our Working Relationship

Never give me work in the morning. Always wait until 5 p.m. and then bring it to me. The challenge of a deadline is refreshing.

If it's really a 'rush job', run in and interrupt me every 10 minutes to ask how it's going. That helps.

Always leave without telling anyone where you're going. It gives me the chance to be creative when somebody asks me where you are.

If you give me more than one job to do, don't tell me which is the priority. Let me guess. It builds management skills and my innate ability of mind-reading.

Do your best to keep me late. I like the office and I really have nowhere to go and nothing else to do. My life is yours.

If a job pleases you, keep it a secret. Leaks like that could cost me a promotion.

If you don't like my work, tell everyone. I like my name to be heard in conversation.

Never introduce me to people you're with. When you refer to them later, my shrewd deductions will identify them.

Tell me all your little problems. No one else has any.

* * *

Letter of Recommendation

I have always found Mr X
working studiously and sincerely at his desk without
idling or gossiping with colleagues. He seldom
wastes his time on useless things and always
finishes assignments on time. He is diligent at
his official work, and can never be found
chitchatting in the canteen. He has absolutely no
vanity in spite of his high accomplishment and
knowledge of his field. I think he can easily be
classed as outstanding, and should on no account be
dispensed with. I strongly feel that Mr X should be
promoted, and a proposal to administration be
sent away as soon as possible.

(Signed)

BRANCH MANAGER

Pinned to the report:

Mr Xxxxx WAS PRESENT WHEN I WAS WRITING THE
REPORT MAILED TO YOU TODAY. KINDLY READ
ONLY THE ALTERNATE LINES 1, 3, 5, 7, etc., FOR
MY TRUE ASSESSMENT OF HIM.

REGARDS,

(Signed)

BRANCH MANAGER

Fun Things to Do in a Lift

Make race-car noises when anyone gets in or out.

Blow your nose and offer to show the contents of
your hankie to other passengers.

Whistle the first seven notes of 'It's a Small World'
incessantly.

Sell Tupperware.

Offer name tags to everyone getting in.

Stand silent and motionless in the corner, facing the wall, without getting out.

Greet everyone getting into the lift with a warm handshake and ask them to call you Admiral.

Fart.

Do Tai Chi exercises.

Stare, grinning, at another passenger for a while, and then announce 'I've got new socks on!'

Give religious tracts to each passenger.

Meow occasionally.

Bet the other passengers you can fit a coin up your nose.

Frown and mutter 'Gotta go, gotta go,' then sigh and say 'Ooops!'

Sing 'Mary Had a Little Lamb' while continually pushing buttons.

Stare at another passenger for a while, then announce: 'You're one of THEM!' and move to the far corner of the lift.

Ask each passenger getting in if you can push the button for them.

Start a singalong.

Play the harmonica.

Shadow box.

Say 'Ding!' at each floor.

Lean against the button panel.

Say 'I wonder what all these do?' and push the red buttons.

Listen to the lift walls with a stethoscope.

Draw a little square on the floor with chalk and announce to the other passengers that this is your 'personal space'.

Take a bite of a sandwich and ask another passenger: 'Wanna see wha in muh mouf?'

Pull your chewing gum out of your mouth in long strings.

Announce in a demonic voice: 'I must find a suitable host body.'

Make explosion noises when anyone presses a button.

Prison vs Work

In prison, you spend the majority of your time in an 8 × 10 cell.
At work, you spend most of your time in a 6 × 8 cubicle.

In prison, you get three meals a day.
At work, you only get a break for one meal and you have to pay for that one.

In prison, you get time off for good behaviour.
At work, you get rewarded for good behaviour with more work.

In prison, a guard locks and unlocks all the doors for you.
At work, you must carry a security card and unlock and open all the doors yourself.

In prison, you can watch TV and play games.
At work, you get fired for watching TV and playing games.

In prison, you get your own toilet.
At work, you have to share.

In prison, they allow your family and friends to visit.
At work, you can't even speak to your family and friends.

In prison, all expenses are paid by taxpayers with no work required.
At work, you get to pay all the expenses to go to work and then they deduct taxes from your salary to pay for prisoners.

In prison, you spend most of your life looking through bars from the inside wanting to get out.

At work, you spend most of your time wanting to get out and go to bars.

In prison, you can join many programs which you can leave at any time.
At work, there are some programs you can never get out of.

In prison, there are sadistic guards.
At work, you have managers.

An Owed to the Spelling Checker

I have a spelling checker
It came with my PC
It plane lee marks four my revue
Miss steaks aye can knot sea.
Eye ran this poem threw it
Your sure reel glad two no
Its vary polished in it's weigh
My checker tolled me sew.
A checker is a bless sing
It freeze yew lodes of thyme

It helps me right awl stiles two reed
And aides me when aye rime.
Each frays come posed up on my screen
Eye trussed too bee a joule
The checker pours o'er every word
To cheque sum spelling rule.
Be fore a veiling checkers
Hour spelling mite decline
And if were lacks or have a laps
We would be maid to wine.
Butt now bee cause my spelling
Is checked with such grate flare
There are know faults with in my cite
Of non eye am a wear.
Now spelling does knot phase me
It does knot bring a tier
My pay purrs awl due glad den
With wrapped words fare as hear.
To rite with care is quite a feet
Of witch won should be proud
And wee mussed dew the best wee can
Sew flaws are knot aloud.

Sow ewe can sea why aye dew prays
Such soft ware four pea seas.
And why I brake in two averse
By righting want too pleas.

'TWAS THE NIGHT BEFORE CHRISTMAS ...

ALL CREATURES GREAT & SMALL

'TWAS THE NIGHT BEFORE CHRISTMAS ...

Staff Memo

Modifications to 'The 12 Days of Christmas' as a consequence of economic rationalism and updated investment policies:

1   The partridge will be retained, but the pear tree, which never produced the cash crop forecast, will be replaced by a plastic hanging plant, providing considerable savings in maintenance.

2   Two turtle doves represent a redundancy that is simply not cost-effective. In addition, their romance during working hours could not be condoned. The positions are, therefore, eliminated.

3   The three French hens have been sold to KFC.

4   The four calling birds will be replaced by an automated voice-mail system, with a call-waiting

option. An analysis is underway to determine who the birds have been calling, how often and how long they talked.

5   The five golden rings have been put on hold. Maintaining a portfolio based on one commodity could have negative implications for institutional investors. Diversification into other precious metals and high-technology stocks appears to be in order.

6   The six geese a-laying constitute a luxury which can no longer be afforded. It has long been felt that the production rate of one egg per goose per day was an example of the general decline in productivity. Three geese will be let go, and an upgrading in the selection procedure by Personnel will assure management that, from now on, every goose it gets will be a good one.

7   The seven swans a-swimming is obviously a number chosen in better times. The function is primarily decorative. Mechanical swans are on order. The current swans will be retrained to learn some new strokes, thereby enhancing their out-placement.

8 As you know, the eight maids a-milking concept has been under heavy scrutiny. A male/female balance in the workforce is being sought. The more militant maids consider this a dead-end job with no upward mobility. Automation of the process may permit the maids to try a-mending, a-mentoring or a-mulching.

9 The nine ladies are growing elderly and, as a result, are finding the dance steps difficult. They are being offered voluntary redundancies.

10 Ten lords a-leaping. We are seeking corporate sponsorship from Toyota.

11 Eleven pipers piping and 12 drummers drumming is a simple case of the band getting too big. A substitution with a string quartet, a cutback on new music and no uniforms will produce savings which will drop right to the bottom line.

Overall we can expect a substantial reduction in assorted people, fowl, animals and related expenses. Though incomplete, studies indicate that stretching deliveries over 12 days is inefficient. If we can deliver in one day, service levels will be improved.

Deeper cuts may be necessary in the future to remain competitive. The Board is currently scrutinising the Snow White division to seek redundancies among the seven dwarfs.

✶ ✶ ✶

The 12 Days of Christmas – Politically Correct Version

On the 12th day of the Eurocentrically imposed midwinter festival, my Significant Other in a consenting, adult, monogamous relationship gave to me:

TWELVE males reclaiming their inner warrior through ritual drumming

ELEVEN pipers piping (plus the 18-member pit orchestra made up of members in good standing of the Musicians Union as called for in their union contract even though they will not be asked to play a note)

TEN melanin-deprived testosterone-poisoned scions of the patriarchal ruling-class system leaping

NINE persons engaged in rhythmic self-expression

EIGHT economically disadvantaged female persons stealing milk products from enslaved bovines

SEVEN endangered swans swimming on protected wetlands

SIX enslaved fowl, producing stolen non-human animal products

FIVE golden symbols of culturally sanctioned enforced domestic incarceration

(Note: After members of the Animal Liberation Front threatened to throw red paint at my computer, the calling birds, French hens and partridge have been reintroduced to their native habitat. To avoid further enslavement, the remaining gift package has been revised.)

FOUR hours of recorded whale songs

THREE deconstructionist poets

TWO Greenpeace calendars printed on recycled processed tree carcasses

and

ONE woodchip activist chained to an old-growth pear tree.

✶   ✶   ✶

The 12 Days of Christmas – E-mail Version

14 December

Dearest Dave,

I went to the door today and the postman delivered a partridge in a pear tree. What a delightful gift. I couldn't have been more surprised.

With dearest love and affection,
Mabel

15 December

Dearest Dave,

Today the postman brought your very sweet gift. Just imagine, two turtle doves ... I'm delighted at your very thoughtful gift. They are just adorable.

All my love,
Mabel

16 December

Dear Dave,

Oh, aren't you the extravagant one! Now I must protest. I don't deserve such generosity. Three French hens. They are just darling but I must insist ... you're too kind.

Love,
Mabel

17 December

Dear Dave,

Today the postman delivered four calling birds. Now really! They are beautiful, but don't you think enough is enough? You're being too romantic.

Affectionately,
Mabel

18 December

Dearest Dave,

What a surprise! Today the postman delivered five golden rings. One for each finger. You're just impossible, but I love it. Frankly, Dave, all those squawking birds were beginning to get on my nerves.

All my love,
Mabel

19 December

Dear Dave,

When I opened the door there were actually six geese a-laying on my front steps. So you're back to the birds again, huh? These geese are huge. Where will I ever keep them? The neighbours are complaining and I can't sleep through the racket. PLEASE STOP!

Cordially,
Mabel

20 December

Dave,

What's with you and those birds??? Seven swans a-swimming. What kind of joke is this? There's bird poop all over the house and they never stop the racket. I'm a nervous wreck and I can't sleep at night. IT'S NOT FUNNY ... So stop with those birds.

Sincerely,
Mabel

21 December

Okay smart arse,

I think I prefer the birds. What am I going to do with eight maids a-milking? It's not enough with all those birds and eight maids a-milking, but they had to bring their own cows. There is manure all over the lawn and I can't move into my own house. Just lay off me.

Mabel

22 December

Hey shithead,

What are you? Some kind of sadist? Now there's nine pipers playing. And, do they play! They haven't stopped chasing those maids since they got here yesterday morning. The cows are upset and are stepping all over those screeching birds. What am I going to do? The neighbours have started a petition to evict me. You'll get yours.

From Mabel

23 December
You rotten bastard,
Now there's ten ladies dancing – I don't know why I call them ladies. They've been with those nine pipers all night long. Now the cows can't sleep and they've got diarrhoea. My living room is a river of brown. The Health Department is trying to evict me.

Yours,
Mabel

24 December
Listen, creep,
What's with the 11 lords a-leaping on those maids and aforementioned 'ladies'? All 234 of the birds are dead. They have been trampled to death. I hope you're satisfied, you rotten swine.

Your sworn enemy,
Miss Mabel Brown

25 December

(from the law offices of Taeker, Spreder & Baegar)

Dear Sir,

This is to acknowledge your latest gift of 12 fiddlers fiddling, which you have seen fit to inflict on our client, Miss Mabel Brown. The destruction, of course, was total. All correspondence should come to our attention. If you should attempt to reach Miss Brown at Happy Dale Sanitorium, the attendants have instructions to shoot you on sight. With this letter, please find attached a warrant for your arrest.

ALL CREATURES GREAT & SMALL

A marine biologist developed a race of genetically engineered dolphins that could live forever if they were fed a steady diet of seagulls.

One day his supply of the birds ran out, so he had to go out and trap some more. On the way back, he spied two lions asleep on the road. Afraid to wake them, he gingerly stepped over them. Immediately he was arrested and charged with transporting gulls across sedate lions for immortal porpoises.

*   *   *

The scene is the tropical waters lapping the Great Barrier Reef. Two prawns are swimming around, one called Justin, the other Christian.

Constantly harassed and threatened by the grey

nurse sharks that patrol the area, the prawns are having a tough time of it. Finally Justin says to Christian: 'I'm sick of being a prawn. I want to be a shark. Then I wouldn't have any worries about being eaten.'

At that very moment a cyclone arrives and, in a flash of lightning, Justin turns into a shark. Christian is horrified and immediately swims off, afraid of being eaten by his old friend.

As time goes on, Justin finds himself becoming bored and lonely as a shark. He has no friends. All his old friends simply swim away whenever he approaches them.

So during the next cyclone Justin prays that the same lightning will strike and change him back into a prawn. And although lightning never strikes twice in the same place, except in stories like this, there is a clap of thunder and a great searing brilliance and, lo and behold, he turns back into a prawn.

With tears of joy in his tiny little eyes Justin swims back to the part of the Barrier Reef where he and Christian used to hang out. And he asks the prawns and coral polyps where his friend might be. 'He's hiding,' they tell him, 'distraught that his best friend became a shark.'

Eager to put things right and end the unhappiness, Justin searches every nook and cranny for Christian. Finally he sees him in a little coral house with a little coral gate and memories come flooding back. He knocks on the gate and shouts: 'It's me, Christian, your old friend. Come out and see me.'

And Christian replies: 'No way! You'll eat me! You're the enemy! A shark! I will not be tricked!'

And Justin cries back: 'No I'm not. That was the old me. I've changed.'

☆   ☆   ☆

Two campers are walking through the bush when they suddenly encounter a huge, slobbering, half-starved dingo. It snarls at them and, licking its canines, advances towards them. They are frozen in their tracks. The first camper whispers: 'I'm glad I wore my running shoes today.'

'It doesn't matter what kind of shoes you're

wearing. You're not going to outrun that dingo,' says the second.

'I don't have to outrun the dingo. I just have to outrun *you*.'

☆　☆　☆

A snail has been unemployed for months and is looking through the paper for a job. He finds one as a vacuum-cleaner salesman. So he goes to his first prospect, knocks on the front door and explains to the owner that he is selling vacuum cleaners. The owner turns around and whacks him one and throws him all the way to the end of the driveway. Six months later, the snail arrives back at the door and asks: 'Why did you do that?'

☆　☆　☆

Two neighbours have been fighting each other for almost four decades. Bob buys a Great Dane and teaches it to go to the dunny in Bill's yard. For one whole year Bill ignores the dog. So Bob then buys a cow and teaches it to go to the dunny in Bill's yard. After about a year-and-a-half of Bob's cow crapping in Bill's yard, being ignored all the time, a semi pulls up in front of Bill's house.

Bob runs over and demands to know what's in the 18-wheeler. 'My new pet elephant,' Bill replies solemnly.

*　　*　　*

Declan the humble crab and Kate the Lobster Princess were madly, deeply and passionately in love. For months they enjoyed an idyllic relationship, until one day Kate scuttled over to Declan in tears. 'We can't see each other any more,' she sobbed.

'Why?' gasped Declan.

'Daddy says that crabs are too common,' she wailed. 'He claims you, a mere crab, and a poor one at that, are the lowest class of crustacean ... and that no daughter of his will marry someone who can only walk sideways.'

Declan was shattered, and scuttled away into

the darkness to drink himself into a filthy state of aquatic oblivion.

That night the great Lobster Ball was taking place. Lobsters came from far and wide, dancing and merrymaking. But the Lobster Princess refused to join in, choosing instead to sit by her father's side, inconsolable. Suddenly the doors burst open, and Declan the crab strode in. The lobsters all stopped their dancing, the Princess gasped and King Lobster rose from his throne.

Slowly and painstakingly, Declan the crab made his way across the floor ... and all could see that he was walking *forwards*, one claw after another! Step by step he made his approach towards the throne, until he finally looked King Lobster in the eye. There was a deathly hush.

Finally the crab spoke: 'Fuck, I'm pissed!'

An old bloke who's been living alone and feeling sad and lonely goes to a pet shop and asks the assistant for a pet that would keep him company through his twilight years while not needing too much care and attention itself.

The shop assistant says: 'I have the very thing, quite special you know,' and produces a cardboard box, inside which is a millipede.

'What's so special about that?' asks the man.

The assistant replies: 'It's a talking millipede.'

The man's very impressed and buys the terrestrial crustacean. Back home he opens the box and asks the millipede: 'Shall we go to the pub then?' But he gets no reply.

He asks the question again but still his new pet says nothing. So he sits back and ponders his acquisition for half an hour and considers taking it back to the pet shop, but decides to give it one more attempt. Looking into the box he again asks: 'Are we going to the pub then?'

The millipede replies: 'All right, for Godsake, don't go on. I'm just putting my shoes on.'

Why did the elephant paint himself all different colours?
So he could hide in the crayon box.

Why is an elephant grey, large and wrinkled?
Because if it were small, round and white, it would be an aspirin.

What would you get if Batman and Robin were run over by a herd of stampeding elephants?
Flatman and Ribbon.

What's the difference between a mosquito and a fly?
A mosquito can fly, but a fly can't mosquito.

☆　☆　☆

One day a young camel decided to ask his father some questions about growing up. 'Daddy, why is it that we have humps on our backs?'

'Well, son, our humps contain fat to sustain us through many days when we are out in the desert.'

'Oh thanks, Dad!' says the youngster. He then asks, 'Daddy, why is it that we have long eyelashes over our eyes?'

'Well son,' says the father, 'in the desert, there are many sandstorms which whip up a lot of sand that can get into our eyes. The long eyelashes protect our eyes from being blinded.'

'Oh thanks, Dad!' says the youngster. 'Daddy, why is it that we have great big padded feet?'

'Well son, in the desert the sand is very soft and we need big feet to be able to walk without our feet sinking into the soft sand.'

'Well thanks, Dad, but what the heck are we doing in London Zoo?'

* * *

Two cows are standing in a field chatting. One cow says: 'Aren't you worried about getting that mad cow disease?'

The other cow says: 'Why should I? I'm a chicken.'

* * *

One day an explorer is out in the jungle. As he wanders along, he comes upon an elephant crying with pain, a large thorn lodged in its foot.

Feeling sorry for the elephant, the man carefully pulls out the thorn. The elephant looks at him gratefully, then limps off into the jungle.

Many years later, the same man visits a circus and sits in the front row. The elephant acts come on and one of the elephants keeps looking over at the explorer.

Eventually, the elephant breaks free, runs over to him ... then picks the man up with his trunk, dashes him to the ground, and tramples him to death with his mighty feet.

Why did the elephant do this?

It wasn't the same elephant.

* * *

There's a chicken and an egg on the bed. The egg is lying there with the biggest grin on his face, smoking a large cigar, and the chicken is sitting there shaking its head in shame. After a while, the egg pipes up and says: 'Well, that solves that question, then.'

*　　*　　*

Two hippos are sitting in some thick, deep, malodorous mud. One says to the other: 'You know the trouble with you? You're lazy. You're fat. You're small. And all you do all day is sit in a swamp.'

And the other says: 'Don't be so bloody hippocritical.'

*　　*　　*

If you have a green ball in one hand and a green ball in the other, what do you have?
Kermit the Frog's undivided attention.

What's pink and hard?
Babe, with a flick-knife.

What do you get when you cross a parrot with a centipede?
A walkie-talkie.

What is green and smells of bacon?
Kermit's finger.

✱ ✱ ✱

A woman is walking down the street on her way to work and sees a parrot in a pet shop. The parrot says to her: 'Hey lady, you are really ugly.'

The woman is furious and storms past the shop.

On her way home she sees the same parrot in the window and the parrot says to her: 'Hey lady, you are really ugly!'

Well, she's incredibly angry now.

The next day she sees the same parrot and the parrot says to her: 'Hey lady, you are really ugly!'

The woman is so annoyed that she goes into the shop and says she will sue the shop and kill the bird. The store manager promises the bird won't say it again.

When the woman walks past the shop the next day the parrot says to her: 'Hey lady!' She pauses and says: 'Yes?'

And the bird says: 'You know.'

★   ★   ★

A man runs into a vet's office carrying his dog, screaming for help. The vet rushes him to an examination room and has him put his dog down on the examination table. The vet examines the still, limp body and after a few moments tells the man that his dog is dead.

The man, clearly agitated and not willing to accept this, demands a second opinion. The vet goes into the back room and comes out with a cat and puts the cat down next to the dog's body. The cat sniffs the body, walking from head to tail poking and sniffing, and finally looks at the vet and meows.

The vet looks at the man and says: 'I'm sorry, but the cat says your dog is dead, too.'

The man, finally resigned to the fate of his dog, thanks the vet and asks how much he owes. The vet answers: 'Three hundred and fifty dollars.'

'Three hundred and fifty dollars to tell me my dog is dead?!' exclaims the man.

'Well,' the vet replies, 'I would have only charged you $50 for my initial diagnosis. The additional $300 was for the cat scan.'

*   *   *

If you can start the day without caffeine

If you can always be cheerful, ignoring aches and pains

If you can resist complaining about your troubles

If you can eat the same food every day and be grateful for it

If you can understand when your loved ones are too busy to give you any time

If you can overlook it when those you love take it out on you when, through no fault of yours, something goes wrong

If you can take criticism and blame without resentment

If you can ignore a friend's limited education and never correct him

If you can resist treating a rich friend better than a poor friend

If you can face the world without lies and deceit

If you can conquer tension without medical help

If you can relax without liquor

If you can sleep without the aid of drugs

If you can say honestly that deep in your heart you have no prejudice against creed, colour, religion or politics ...

then you're a dog.

DAD & DAVE & MABEL

DAD & DAVE & MABEL

Dave came home to find a total stranger in bed with Mabel. So he rushed outside and grabbed his shotgun.

'It's all right, it's all right,' said the stranger. 'I'm a doctor, I'm a doctor! And I've been taking Mabel's temperature.'

Dave pulled back the hammers on the shotgun. 'Well, you better have numbers on that thing when you take it out.'

* * *

Dave and Mabel came to Melbourne for the Royal Show. But before they could book into their cheap hotel they were mugged in Swanston Street. All they were left with was one cheque form.

Dave decided to turn this to their advantage.

Because he'd never learnt to write, he asked Mabel to write '9' on the cheque form and 'put some noughts after it'.

Mabel followed instructions and wrote a cash cheque for $900.

'No,' said Dave, 'it needs more noughts.'

'Why am I doing this?' asked Mabel.

'So we can go to a good hotel, give them a cheque and ask them to put it in the safe. They'll think we're very rich and give us the bridal suite and we'll be able to order some tucker from room service.'

So Mabel kept adding noughts until Dave was satisfied – and she presented the hotel with a cheque for $9 million.

The receptionist looked at the cheque and looked at Dave and Mabel. Then she called the bouncer and had them chucked out into the street.

Dave was furious with Mabel. 'You should have added some more of them noughts.'

Dad staggered into the stables where Dave was working on the ute. 'What's wrong, son?' Dad asked.

'Piston broke,' said Dave.

'So am I,' muttered Dad as he stumbled off.

Dave was visiting Paris with Mabel. Standing outside Notre Dame cathedral they saw a magnificent wedding procession enter. 'Who's the bridegroom?' Dave asked a Frenchman standing next to him.

'Je ne sais pas,' was the reply.

A few minutes later, Dave and Mabel were inside the cathedral looking at the famous rose window – and saw a coffin being carried down the far aisle.

'Whose funeral?' he asked a nun.

'Je ne sais pas,' said the nun.

'Bugger me,' Dave said to Mabel. 'He didn't last long.'

Dad and Dave were at a country race meeting wondering what horse to back. Overhearing their conversation, a grizzled old cocky said: 'I'd back mine.'

'What's its name?' asked Dave.

'Humdinger,' said the old cocky.

'And is it?'

'Abso-bloody-lutely. Humdinger is the best damn horse this country's ever seen. I took the old girl to the Melbourne Cup last year and they all laughed at me. But once the starting gates were open she rushed out and led the lot of them. Which was no surprise to me. But, on the back stretch, I noticed her hesitate. And then and there she dropped a foal.'

'Well,' said Dad, 'you can't win them all.'

'No,' said Dave, 'you'd have to forgive her losing.'

'Who said anything about losing? Humdinger never lost. She had the foal. And she still won the race by five lengths. And the foal came in second.'

Dave arrived at the town hall for the Annual Gala Dance and, tripping on the front stairs, tore one knee of his trousers.

'Come into the ladies' dressing room,' said Mabel, 'there's no one there and I'll pin the tear for you.'

But the tear was too large to be pinned. Fortunately Mabel had a needle and thread in her handbag. Instructing Dave to remove his pants, she told him to hold the door handle tightly so no one could get in.

No sooner had she started sewing when a group of women could be heard outside the door – and they began trying to get in. 'Let us in! Let us in!' they cried. 'Mrs Briggs is ill.'

Mabel put down the torn trousers and said to Dave: 'Quick, get into this closet.'

She opened the door and pushed Dave through it just in time. And in rushed the women with the ailing Mrs Briggs.

Whereupon there was pounding from the door of the closet. 'Let me in! Let me in!' screamed Dave.

'But the women are here,' said Mabel.

'Fuck the women!' yelled Dave. 'I'm out in the bloody ballroom!'

✲　✲　✲

Dave and Mabel were invited to a fancy-dress party, a fundraiser for a fashionable illness. But at the last minute Mabel claimed a headache and told Dave to go alone.

But she had a plan. After he'd left dressed as Donald Duck, Mabel donned her costume, a stunning Venetian outfit, complete with mask, and headed for the venue.

And there he was, cavorting around on the dance floor, dancing with every woman in sight, copping a little feel here and a little kiss there.

In due course, she sidled up and began flirting with him outrageously. And he obviously didn't have a clue as to who was behind the mask. So next thing he invited her to the carpark where he gave her a knee-trembler against a shadowed wall.

Just before the unmasking at midnight she slipped away and went home and packed the costume in its box and climbed into bed, wondering what he'd have to say for himself.

Mabel was sitting up reading when Dave arrived. 'Hello darling, did you have a good time?'

And Dave said: 'No, not really. I never have a good time when you're not with me.'

So she asked: 'Did you dance much?'

And he said: 'I didn't even dance once. When I got there I met Pete and Bill and some of the other blokes and we went into a back room and played poker all evening. But you're not going to believe what happened to the bloke I loaned my costume to.'

E

TERMS OF EMPLOYMENT

TERMS OF EMPLOYMENT

They'd been downsizing in the company and now the manager was in a quandary. He had to sack one more person, and it was down to Debra or Jack.

It would be a difficult decision to make because both were equally qualified and did excellent work.

He decided that, next morning, whichever one went to the toilet first would have to go. And that turned out to be Debra, who'd been partying all night and was still half pissed. So the manager approached her and said: 'Debra, I've got bad news. I have to lay you or Jack off.'

And Debra replied: 'Would you mind jacking off? I've got a terrible headache.'

* * *

Things to Say if You're Caught Sleeping at Your Desk

They told me at the blood bank this might happen.

Phew! I left the top off the white-out. You probably got here just in time.

I was testing my keyboard for drool resistance.

Damn! Why did you interrupt me? I'd almost figured out the solution to our biggest problem.

... in Jesus's name, Amen.

Seeking to inspire the staff, the boss had the personnel manager place a sign directly above the sink in the men's toilets. It had just one word on it: THINK!

The next day the boss was in the toilet and saw that there was a second sign right below the first, just above the soap dispenser. A sign with one word: THOAP!

Bill worked in a pickle factory. He had been employed there for a number of years when he came home one day to confess to his wife that he had a terrible compulsion. He had an urge to stick his penis into the pickle slicer. His wife suggested that he should see a sex therapist to talk about it, but Bill indicated that he'd be too embarrassed. He vowed to overcome the compulsion on his own.

One day, a few weeks later, Bill came home absolutely ashen. His wife could see at once that something was seriously wrong. 'What's wrong, Bill?' she asked.

'Do you remember that I told you how I had this tremendous urge to put my penis into the pickle slicer?'

'Oh, Bill, you didn't?'

'Yes, I did.'

'My God, Bill, what happened?'

'I got fired.'

'No, Bill. I mean what happened with the pickle slicer?'

'Oh, she got fired too.'

✷ ✷ ✷

Graffiti from a Corporate Dunny

Eagles may soar, but weasels don't get sucked into jet engines.

Doing a job RIGHT the first time gets the job done. Doing the job WRONG 14 times gives you job security.

Rome did not create a great empire by having meetings; they did it by killing all those who opposed them.

We put the 'k' in 'kwality'.

If something doesn't feel right, you're not feeling the right thing.

Artificial Intelligence is no match for Natural Stupidity.

A person who smiles in the face of adversity ... probably has a scapegoat.

If you can stay calm, while all around you is

chaos ... then you probably haven't completely understood the situation.

Plagiarism saves time.

If at first you don't succeed, try management.

Never put off until tomorrow what you can avoid altogether.

TEAMWORK means never having to take all the blame yourself.

The beatings will continue until morale improves.

Never underestimate the power of very stupid people in large groups.

We waste time, so you don't have to hang in there, retirement is only 30 years away!

Go the extra mile. It makes your boss look like an incompetent slacker.

A snooze button is a poor substitute for no alarm clock at all.

When the going gets tough, the tough take a coffee break.

INDECISION is the key to FLEXIBILITY.

Succeed in spite of management.

Aim low, reach your goals, avoid disappointment.

We waste more time by 8.00 in the morning than other companies do all day.

You pretend to work, and we'll pretend to pay you.

Work: It isn't just for sleeping any more.

☆   ☆   ☆

A Handy Guide to Job Placement

Take the prospective employees you are trying to place and put them in a room with only a table and two chairs. Leave them alone for two hours. Provide no instructions. Not even a hint. At the end of that time go back and see what they are doing.

- If they've taken the table apart, put them in Engineering.
- If they're counting the butts in the ashtray, assign them to Accounting.
- If they're yelling and waving their arms, send them off to Manufacturing.
- If they're talking to the chairs, Personnel is a good spot for them.
- If they are sleeping, they are Management material.
- If they don't even look up when you enter the room, assign them to Security.
- If they try to tell you it's not as bad as it looks, send them to Marketing.
- And if they've left early, they're already in Sales.

* * *

After the annual Christmas party John woke up with a pounding headache, completely unable to recall the events of the previous evening. After an unsteady trip to the bathroom he was able to make his way downstairs, where his wife put a cup of coffee in front of him. 'Darling,' he moaned, 'tell me what went on last night. Was it as bad as I think it might have been?'

'Even worse,' she told him. 'You made a complete arse of yourself. You succeeded in antagonising the entire board of directors. You insulted the chairman of the company to his face.'

'Well, he's an arrogant, self-important prick. I wouldn't bother pissing on him.'

'Well, you did. All over his suit. And he fired you.'

'Well, fuck him!' said John.

'I did, darling. You're back at work on Monday.'

Definition of a Consultant

A guy who can tell you a thousand ways to make love – but doesn't know any women.

FAIRY STORIES

FAIRY STORIES

Pinocchio's girlfriend complains of splinters. Pinocchio's father, the old carpenter, says to his son: 'Well, you better give yourself a rub-down prior to sex.'

'What do you mean, father?'

'If you want to prevent splinters, rub your wooden penis with fine sandpaper.'

A few weeks later, the old carpenter asks his wooden son: 'How's your girlfriend?'

Pinocchio says: 'Who needs a girlfriend?'

Cinderella wants to go to the ball, but her wicked stepmother won't let her. As Cinderella sits crying in the garden, her fairy godmother appears and promises to provide Cinderella with everything she needs to go to the ball, but only on two conditions.

'First, you must wear a diaphragm.' Cinderella agrees, then says: 'What's the second condition?'

'You must be home by 2 a.m. Any later and your diaphragm will turn into a pumpkin.'

Cinderella agrees to be home by 2 a.m. The appointed hour comes and goes, and Cinderella doesn't show up.

Finally, at 5 a.m., Cinderella arrives, looking lovestruck and very satisfied.

'Where have you been?' demands the fairy godmother. 'Your diaphragm was supposed to turn into a pumpkin three hours ago!'

'I met a prince, Fairy Godmother. He took care of everything.'

'I know of no prince with that kind of power! Tell me his name!'

'I can't remember, exactly ... Peter Peter, something or other ...'

Snow White saw Pinocchio walking through the woods so she ran up behind him, knocked him flat on his back, and then sat on his face crying: 'Lie to me! Lie to me!'

*　*　*

Mickey Mouse and Minnie Mouse were in the divorce court and the judge said to Mickey: 'You say here that your wife is crazy.'

Mickey replied: 'No I didn't. I said she's fucking Goofy.'

*　*　*

On a farm in Far North Queensland lived a man and a woman and their three sons. Early one morning, the woman awoke, and while looking out the window, she saw that the family's only cow was lying dead in the paddock. The situation looked hopeless to her – how could she possibly continue to feed her family now? In a depressed state of mind, she hanged herself.

When the man awoke to find his wife dead, as well as the cow, he too began to see the hopelessness of the situation, and he shot himself in the head.

Now, the oldest son woke up to discover his parents dead (and the cow!) and he decided to go down to the river and drown himself. When he got to the river, he found a mermaid sitting on the bank. She said: 'I have seen all and know the reason for your despair. But if you will have sex with me five times in a row, then I will restore your parents and the cow to you.' The son agreed to try, but after four times, he was simply unable to get it up again. So the mermaid drowned him in the river.

Next the second son woke up. After discovering what had happened, he too decided to throw himself into the river. The mermaid said to him: 'If you will have sex with me ten times in a row, then I will make everything right.' And while the son tried his best (seven times!), it was not enough to satisfy the mermaid, so she drowned him in the river.

The third son was overwhelmed by the tragedy of it all. He decided that life was a hopeless prospect and he too went down to the river to throw himself in. And there he also met the mermaid, who said: 'I have seen all that has happened, and I can make everything right if you will only have sex with me 15 times in a row!' The young man replied: 'Is that all? Why not 20 times in a row?' The mermaid was somewhat taken aback at this request. Then he said: 'Hell, why not 25 times in a row?' And even as she was reluctantly agreeing to his request, he said: 'Why not 30 times in a row!?'

Finally she said: 'Enough! Okay, if you will have sex with me 30 times in a row, then I will bring everybody back to perfect health.'

Then the young son said: 'Well, hold on just a minute. How do I know that 30 times in a row won't kill you like it did the cow?'

GENDER WARS

GOLF WAR

GENDER WARS

Why do men whistle while on the toilet?
So they know which end to wipe.

Why can't little girls fart?
They don't have an arsehole until they get married.

What's a man's idea of helping to make the bed?
Getting out of it.

What can a bird do that a man can't?
Whistle through its pecker.

Why don't women blink during foreplay?
They don't have time.

Why did God put men on earth?
Because a vibrator can't mow the lawn.

What do electric trains and breasts have in common?
They're intended for children, but it's men who usually end up playing with them.

Why were men given larger brains than dogs?
So they wouldn't hump women's legs at cocktail parties.

Why do men come so quickly?
So they can rush down to the pub and tell their mates.

What's the definition of a bachelor pad?
A flat where the plants are all dead but there's something growing in the fridge.

Why are men like toilets?
They're either vacant, engaged or full of crap.

What's the definition of making love?
It's what a woman does while a man's screwing her.

Women have many faults. Men, however, have only two: everything they say and everything they do.

Adam came first, but then, men always do.

* * *

Great Reasons to Be a Bloke

Phone conversations are over in 30 seconds.

You know stuff about eight-cylinder engines.

A five-day holiday needs only one suitcase.

You can open all your own jars.

It doesn't cost you as much for a haircut.

You can kill your own food.

Everything on your face stays its original colour.

Grey hair and wrinkles add character.

If another bloke shows up at a party in the same outfit, who gives a fuck?

You're not expected to know the names of more than five colours.

The same hairstyle lasts for years, maybe decades.

You don't have to shave below your neck.

★   ★   ★

You're a Redneck if ...

You think that a slice of ham on a Sao is an hors d'oeuvre.

You consider a six-pack and a bug zapper high-quality entertainment.

Fewer than half your cars run.

Your mum doesn't remove the Marlboro from her lips before telling the motorcycle cop to kiss her arse.

The primary colour of your car is filler.

You think that women are turned on by animal noises and seductive tongue gestures.

Your family tree doesn't fork.

Your wife's hairdo has been ruined by a ceiling fan.

Your front porch collapses and more than six dogs are killed.

Your home has more miles on it than your car.

Your brother-in-law is your uncle.

You prominently display gifts bought at Graceland.

The diploma hanging in your study contains the words 'Trucking Institute'.

Your favourite Christmas present was a painting on black velvet.

You think that Dom Perignon is a Mafia leader.

The most commonly heard phrase at your family reunion is 'What the hell are you looking at, shithead?'

You have a rag for a petrol cap.

You have to go outside to get something out of the fridge.

You've ever financed a tattoo.

Your idea of a seven-course meal is a bucket of KFC and a six-pack.

You have spray-painted your girlfriend's name on an overpass.

You have been too drunk to fish.

You have to remove a toothpick for wedding pictures.

The directions to your house include: 'Turn off the made road'.

You've lost at least one tooth opening a beer bottle.

You consider your number plate personalised because your dad made it in prison.

You've been fired from a construction job because of your appearance.

✱ ✱ ✱

Her Story

Ed was in an odd mood last night. I thought it might have been because I arrived a bit late at the bar. He didn't say anything much about it, but the conversation was quite slow-going. So I thought we should go somewhere more intimate so we could talk more privately. We headed for our favourite restaurant but he was still a bit funny and I couldn't cheer him up. And I started to wonder whether it was me. So I asked him, and he said no. But I wasn't really sure. So anyway, in the cab back to his flat I said that I loved him and he just put his arm around me and stared out the window. By the time we got to his place I was worried that he was going off me. And I tried to ask him about it but he just switched on the TV. So I said that I was going to sleep and after about ten minutes he climbed into bed and we had sex. But he seemed quite bored afterwards. I really wanted to leave. I don't know. I just don't know

what he thinks any more. I mean, do you think he's met someone else?

His Story

Shit day at work. Great shag later.

★　★　★

One day a woman was walking to her favourite cafe in San Francisco on her lunch break when she saw a lamp resembling the one in *Aladdin* lying in an alley. She picked it up and rubbed it, and sure enough out came a genie. The genie told her she would grant the woman one wish. After thinking for a good five minutes, the woman said: 'I want a bridge to be built from San Francisco to Hawaii so I can drive there every weekend.'

The genie responded: 'From San Francisco to Hawaii?!? Do you know how long it would take to build that, and how much taxes would go up on road repairs, and how many people would have to work on it each year ...' the genie went on and on until finally the woman interrupted, 'Okay, okay, I'll make another wish!' The genie was ecstatic. 'Thank you SOOO much!'

After thinking for a few minutes the woman told the genie: 'I wish to be able to understand the male brain, to know why they do what they do.'

Within seconds the genie responded: 'Would you like that bridge two lanes or four?'

★ ★ ★

What do you say to a woman with no arms and no legs?
Nice tits.

Which of the following doesn't belong? Wife, meat, eggs, blow job?
The blow job. You can beat your wife, your eggs or your meat but you can't beat a blow job.

What's the difference between a woman and a volcano?
A volcano doesn't fake eruptions.

What's the difference between a dog scratching at the door and a woman ringing the bell?
When you let the dog in it'll stop whining.

Why don't women fart as much as men?
They can't shut their mouths long enough to build up the pressure.

What's the best way to stop the noise in your car?
Let her drive.

What's the difference between a penis and a bonus?
Your wife will always blow your bonus.

How to Impress a Woman

Compliment her
Cuddle her
Kiss her

Caress her
Love her
Stroke her
Tease her
Comfort her
Protect her
Hug her
Hold her
Spend money on her
Wine and dine her
Buy things for her
Listen to her
Care for her
Stand by her
Support her
Go to the ends of the earth for her.

How to Impress a Man

Show up naked
Bring beer.

That's a really beautiful fur coat,' said Lynda Stoner to a woman in the street. 'But don't you pity the poor beast who suffered so that you might have it?'

The woman replied: 'Why do you ask? Do you know my husband?'

*   *   *

Seminars for Women (prepared and presented by men)

Elementary Map Reading

Crying and Law Enforcement

Advanced Maths Seminar: Programming Your VCR

You CAN Go Shopping for Less than Four Hours

Gaining Five Pounds vs The End of the World: A Study in Contrast

The Seven-outfit Week

PMS: It's YOUR Problem, Not Mine (formerly It's

Happened Monthly Since Puberty, Deal With It)

Driving I: Getting Past Automatic Transmissions
Driving II: The Meaning of Blinking Red Lights
Driving III: Approximating a Constant Speed
Driving IV: Make-up and Driving: Oil and Water

How to Earn Your Own Money

Gift-giving Fundamentals (formerly titled: Fabric Bad, Electronics Good)

Putting the Seat Down by Yourself: Potential Energy Is on Your Side

Know When to Say When: The Limits of Make-up

Beyond 'Clean and Dirty': The Nuances of Wearable Laundry

Yes, You Can Buy Condoms (formerly We Learned to Deal with the Embarrassment)

What Goes Around Comes Around: Why His Credit Card is Not a Toy

The Penis: His Best Friend Can Be Yours Too

Commitment Schmittment (formerly Wedlock Schmedlock)

To Honour and Obey: Remembering the Small Print above 'I Do'

Why Your Mother Is Unwelcome in the House

Your Mate: Selfish Bastard, or Victimised Sensitive Man?

✶   ✶   ✶

What Am I?

A useful tool, commonly found in the range of eight inches long, the functioning of which is enjoyed by members of both sex.

It is usually found hung, dangling loosely, ready for instant action.

It boasts a clump of little hairy things at one end and a small hole at the other.

In use, it is inserted, almost always willingly, sometimes slowly, sometimes quickly, into a warm, fleshy, moist opening where it is thrust in and drawn out again and again, many times in succession, often quickly and accompanied by squirming bodily movement.

Anyone found listening in will most surely recognise the rhythmic, pulsing sound, resulting from the well-lubricated movements.

When finally withdrawn, it leaves behind a juicy, frothy, sticky white substance, some of which will need cleaning from the outer surfaces of the opening and some from its long glistening shaft.

After everything is done and the flowing and cleansing liquids have ceased emanating, it is returned to its freely hanging state of rest, ready for yet another bit of action, hopefully reaching its bristling climax twice or three times a day. But often much less.

What am I?

The answer to the riddle is none other than your very own ... toothbrush!

(What were you thinking? You PERVERT!)

I've got a head I can't think with.
An eye I can't see out of.
I have to hang around with two nuts all the time.
My closest neighbour is an arsehole.
My owner beats me repeatedly.
And I have to wear this rubber suit.
And throw up all over myself.

It isn't easy being a dick.

GOLF WAR

Bob arrived at the first tee at Royal Melbourne to play with his regular partners. He took his driver and amazed his mates by sending the ball down the fairway as if he were Greg Norman. After all, Bob had a 24-handicap.

A few minutes later he took out a short iron and knocked it into the middle of the green and proceeded to calmly 2-putt for par. His mates shook their heads in astonishment.

And Bob kept playing brilliantly – for the next five holes even par through six.

The seventh was a long, difficult par four of some 420 metres. Once again, straight down the middle!

'Okay, okay,' said his friends. 'What's going on?'

He explained that he'd just got new bifocal specs

and when he looked down at the ball he could see a big club and a little club, a big ball and a little ball. So he hit the little ball with the big club!

And that's the way the game went, with Bob saying: 'See! Big club, little club. Big ball, little ball. I hit the little ball with the big club – easy!'

And it was the same with putting. His putts were astonishing. 'It's easy! I see a big ball and a little ball ... see a big hole and a little hole. So I hit the little ball into the big hole.'

On the next hole he left the group for a few moments and disappeared into the rough. On his return they could see that his slacks were wet with pee. 'What happened, Bob?'

'Well, I went into the bush for a quick leak and when I looked down I saw a big one and a little one. I knew the big one wasn't mine, so I put it away.'

After a very, very bad round of golf Paddy went home and beat his wife to death. Feeling a bit guilty he rang the police and confessed. A few minutes later a police car screeched up the driveway and two cops banged on the door.

Paddy let them in and the police inspected the corpse.

Police: 'She's your wife?'

Paddy: 'Yes.'

Police: 'And you killed her?'

Paddy: 'Yes.'

Police: 'How did you kill her?'

Paddy: 'I beat her to death with my one iron.'

Police: 'How many times did you actually hit her?'

Paddy: 'Seven – but put me down for five.'

* * *

An arrogant American is playing a round with a business client and continually abuses his caddy. At the sixth hole – 170 metres over water – he demands of the caddy 'What club do I use here?' The caddy replies: 'Well, when President Bush played here with Prime Minister Hawke, they both used a six iron.'

As rude as ever, the golfer grabs the six iron,

hits the ball and it lands in the middle of the pond. 'Hey, you bastard! You gave me a six iron and it obviously wasn't enough. I went right into the water!'

And the caddy replies: 'That's what the President and Prime Minister did, too.'

A beautiful, bountiful blonde arrives at her golf course and, rather than playing alone, joins a threesome of blokes. With the help of their tips she arrives at the 18th hole lying 98 with a 2-metre putt left to break 100.

'I have never broken 100 since I started playing golf two years ago,' she says excitedly. 'And I'm so anxious to break 100 that whichever one of you gives me the best tip on how to sink the putt will be rewarded. I'll let him make love to me right here on the green!'

There is great excitement. The first guy checks the lines and breaks from all sides and suggests she borrow 1 metre right at the hole, 'and just strike it hard enough to drop it in'.

The second guy agrees, but tells her to hit it firm and slam dunk it. She turns round to hear the advice of the third bloke – only to find him stark naked. 'But you haven't even given me your tip!'

To which he replies: 'Pick it up! It's a gimme.'

A couple of brothers, one eight years old, one six, were playing golf with their friends. And while practising golf they were also practising swearing. The eight-year-old said that after the game they should try out their new vocabulary on Mum. 'When we go back to the clubhouse I'll say "Hell", he tells his little brother, 'and you say "Arse".' The six-year-old agreed.

They were back in the clubhouse for snacks when their mother came in. 'How did the game go?'

The eight-year-old replied: 'Hell, Mum. It was good except I got a triple bogey.'

The mother reacted with a swift whack on the boy's bum – and he ran off crying and rubbing his backside.

With a sterner voice the mother asked her younger son how his game had gone. And he replied: 'Not bad, but you can bet your arse I didn't get a triple bogey!'

A young golfer decided he just had time to sneak in nine holes before going home. As he was about to tee off an elderly golfer asked if he could join him. Not wishing to be rude, the young man agreed and off they went.

To his surprise the senior moved quite well. He didn't hit far but walked fast between shots. On the last hole the young man pulled his drive and it went into the rough behind a 7-metre tree. He suggested he punch it out, but the senior said: 'When I was your age I could hit over the top of that tree.'

Accepting the challenge the young man took out a seven iron, took a hefty swing and hit the top of the tree. As they walked away the old man said: 'Of course, when I was your age the tree was only 2 metres tall.'

* * *

The boss asked a young exec. to take some clients to the golf club. The exec. was delighted, played 18 holes with the guests, had a few beers and laughs in the clubhouse and then drove home, only to find his wife in bed with the boss! He immediately returned to the clubhouse and the waiter said: 'I thought you went home!'

'Yes,' he said, 'but I found my wife in bed with the boss and as they're in the early stages I reckoned I might be able to fit in another nine.'

* * *

Two couples played golf together regularly, and on the sixth hole, a par four, one of the foursome invariably hit her ball into the water. She did it every time.

The others recommended that she see a hypno-therapist so that she wouldn't be psyched out by the presence of water.

The therapist hypnotised her and planted

suggestions that when playing the second shot on the sixth hole she wouldn't see water. Instead she'd see a plush green fairway leading all the way up to the green.

A year later someone at the club asked what had become of the woman. After all, she hadn't been seen playing golf at the club for months. 'It was very, very sad,' said a caddy. 'She drowned at the par-four sixth.'

Jack was a moderately successful golfer, but as he got older he was increasingly hampered by incredible headaches. His golf, personal hygiene and love life started to suffer. When his game turned really sour he sought medical help. After being referred from one specialist to another, he finally came across a doctor who solved the problem.

'The good news is I can cure your headaches; the bad news is that it will require castration. You have a very rare condition which causes your testicles to press up against the base of your spine. The pressure creates one hell of a headache. The only way to relieve the pressure and allow your swing to work again is to remove the testicles.'

Jack was shocked and depressed. He wondered if he had anything to live for, but then figured at least he could play reasonable golf again. He decided he had no choice but to go under the knife. When he left the hospital, his mind was clear but he felt like he was missing an important part of himself. As he walked down the street, he realised that he felt like a different person. He could make a new beginning, swing free and live a new life. He went to the club for a drink and as he walked past the pro shop he thought: 'That's what I need – a new outfit!'

He entered the shop and told the salesman, 'I'd like some new golf slacks.' The salesman eyed him briefly and said, 'Let's see … size 44 long.'

Jack laughed. 'That's right! How did you know?'

'It's my job.'

Jack tried on the slacks and they fitted perfectly. As Jack admired himself in the mirror, the salesman asked, 'How about a new shirt? I've got some great new Greg Norman stock.'

Jack thought for a moment, and then said: 'Sure.' The salesman eyed Jack and said, 'Let's see. Thirty-four sleeve and ... 16-and-a-half neck.'

Jack was surprised. 'That's right! How did you know?'

'It's my job.'

Jack tried on the shirt, and it fitted perfectly. As Jack adjusted the collar in the mirror, the salesman asked: 'How about new shoes? We've got new stock with soft spikes.'

Jack was on a roll and agreed. The salesman said: 'Let's see ... nine-and-a-half, wide.'

Jack was astonished. 'That's right! How did you know?'

'It's my job.'

Jack tried on the shoes and they fitted perfectly. Jack walked comfortably around the shop and the salesman asked: 'How about a new hat?'

Without hesitating, Jack said: 'Sure ...' The salesman eyed Jack's head and said: 'Let's see ... 60.'

Jack was really impressed. 'That's right! How did you know?'

'It's my job.'

The hat fitted perfectly. Jack was feeling great when the salesman asked: 'How about some new underwear? Got some great new imported stock.' Jack thought for a second and said: 'Sure.'

The salesman stepped back, eyed Jack's waist and said, 'Let's see ... size 36.'

Jack laughed. 'No, I've worn size 34 since I was 18 years old.'

The salesman shook his head. 'You can't wear a size 34 – every time you swing, it would press your testicles up against the base of your spine and give you one hell of a headache.'

★　　★　　★

Three golfers are standing at the gates of heaven and St Peter asks them if they ever cheated while playing golf with their wives.

The first man says: 'All the time.' So St Peter gives him a Harley Davidson and admits him to heaven.

The second man says: 'I cheated a couple of times.' So St Peter gives him a BMW and lets him into heaven.

The third man says: 'For 40 years I only ever played golf with my wife. Most of the time she beat me, but I never cheated.' So St Peter gives him a Rolls Royce and admits him to heaven.

A week later the three men meet at an intersection in heaven and the third man is sitting in his car crying. The other men ask why he's crying – he has such a nice car. The third man says: 'I just saw my wife and she's driving a skateboard.'

After years of excluding Jews, a famous golf club is embarrassed by bad publicity and admits a famous Jewish businessman to membership. Immensely rich (high on the *BRW* top 100), he's very pleased by the turn of events and arrives for his first round. And he asks the pro: 'Do your caddies cater for special needs?'

The pro replies: 'Yes, we've got caddies who specialise in helping the left-handed, the half-blind, the lame, the slicers.'

'Well, I want a caddy who can work "Jewish-style".'

The pro asks the caddies if anyone feels qualified. After a long silence a new caddy says that he does. On the way to the first tee he confesses: 'I really don't know how to caddy Jewish-style but wanted to impress the others. But if you show me I'll do it for half-price.'

To which the man replies: 'You learn fast!'

* * *

Mum was waiting for her ten-year-old to return from his Sunday golf match at the public course. When he arrived he was absolutely filthy and covered in green slime. 'How did you get yourself in such a mess?! Did you hit a ball into the water?'

'No, Mum. But when we were passing the creek on the 17th we saw some frogs. So we started bombing them with golf balls. And then we put firecrackers up their arse.'

'Rectum, Tommy,' Mum said reprovingly, 'rectum!'

And Tommy said, 'Blood oath we did!'
And he wiped at the green slime.

*　　*　　*

Two friends are playing golf together at the Logan
City Golf Course in Brisbane. One of them lands
on a dirt track covered in gravel and sunken stones.
The owner of the ball asks his friend: 'Do you mind
if I have a drop? I can't play from here, it's too
rough.'

'Sorry, but you play from where you lie!'

'But I'm going to wreck my club. It's all rocks
and gravel.'

'No favours. You play from where you lie.'

The poor chap stops arguing and takes a trial
swing. Gravel and sparks fly everywhere. Second
swing, same again. Finally he feels ready, moves to
the ball and hits ... gravel and sparks everywhere,
but the fall flies off beautifully, lands on the green
and stops inches from the cup.

'My God, what a shot! Which club did you use?'

'Your five iron.'

* * *

A lady newcomer to golf is on the first tee and asks her pro: 'So, what do I do now?'

The pro replies: 'See that flag on the green? You have to hit your ball as close to it as you can.'

The lady lets fly with a mighty swipe and the ball comes to rest 8 centimetres from the hole. She asks: 'What do I do now?'

The pro answers: 'You're supposed to hit it in the hole.'

The woman screams: 'Why didn't you tell me that before?'

* * *

A usually happy weekend golfer comes home from his game very late and much the worse for wear. His wife greets him at the door and demands: 'Where the hell have you been, and what have you been doing?'

The husband wobbles around and slurs: 'Had a bad game, sort of lost everything. You'd better pack some bags. I even lost you.'

The wife screams: 'How could you do that?'

'It wasn't easy,' the bloke replies. 'I had to miss three one-foot putts in the last four holes.'

☆ ☆ ☆

A husband and wife play golf together every day. She always wins. Tired of humiliation, he decides to break her concentration. As she readies to tee off he goes up to her and whispers into her ear: 'I've had a mistress for the whole 15 years we've been married.'

Needless to say, the wife loses the round.

Next day, the wife decides it's time to punish her husband. As he readies to tee off she says: 'Before we met I was a man.'

He loses the round.

At work the next day he just can't get over what his wife has told him. A colleague notices his distress and the husband blurts out the whole story.

'Why worry?' says the colleague. 'You love your wife and have been happy for 15 years. Just forget the whole thing.'

'That's not the point,' says the husband. 'She's been teeing off the women's tee for all that time!'

Ten Things in Golf that Sound Dirty

1 Look at the size of his putter.
2 Oh shit, my shaft's all bent.
3 You really whacked the hell out of that sucker.
4 After 18 holes I can barely walk.
5 My hands are so sweaty I can't get a good grip.
6 Lift your head and spread your legs.
7 You have a nice stroke, but your follow-through leaves a lot to be desired.
8 Just turn your back and drop it.
9 Hold up, I've got to wash my balls.
10 Damn, I missed the hole again.

During a ladies' tournament a woman slices the

ball so badly that it sails across the creek, narrowly missing a young blonde playing an entirely different hole. 'How do I get to the other side?' the woman calls.

Looking somewhat confused, the blonde calls back: 'You're already on the other side!'

A couple of friends were playing a round on a remote course in Arnhem Land. After several holes one of them needed to pee and so walked into the rough and unzipped. Whereupon an enormous taipan appeared from nowhere and bit it. He screamed for help and the snake slithered away. He explained to his friend what had happened. His friend rushed back to the clubhouse, found a doctor teeing off and asked what could be done. The doctor told him to make a small cut beside the bite and to suck and suck until all the poison was removed. He thanked the doctor and ran back to his friend.

'What did the doctor say?'

'Bad news. You're going to die.'

＊　＊　＊

Four golfers were discussing how they got their wives to let them play.

The first golfer said he sent his wife a dozen red roses and made a gourmet dinner for two.

The second golfer said he promised to do all of the vacuuming, dusting and laundry.

The third golfer said he painted the kitchen, the lounge room and the bedroom.

The fourth golfer said it was very simple. He set the alarm for 5.30 a.m. and when he woke up he rolled over and asked his wife: 'Intercourse or golf course?' And his wife always replied: 'Don't forget your sweater.'

＊　＊　＊

The Pope met with his cardinals to discuss a proposal from Benjamin Netanyahu.

'Your Holiness,' said one of the cardinals. 'Mr Netanyahu wants to challenge you to a game of golf to show the friendship and ecumenical spirit shared by the Jewish and Catholic faiths.'

The Pope thought it was a good idea, but he had never held a golf club in his life. 'Have we not,' he asked, 'a cardinal who can represent me against the leader of Israel?'

'None that plays golf very well,' a cardinal said. 'But there is a man named Jack Nicklaus, an American golfer, who is a devout Catholic. We can offer to make him a cardinal; then ask him to play Benjamin Netanyahu as your personal representative. In addition to showing our spirit of cooperation, we'll be sure to win the match.'

Everyone agreed it was a good idea.

The call was made. Of course, Nicklaus was honoured and agreed to play.

The day after the match, Nicklaus reported to the Vatican to inform the Pope of the result. 'I have some good news and some bad news, Your Holiness,' said the world-class golfer.

'Tell me the good news first, Cardinal Nicklaus,' said the Pope.

'Well, Your Holiness, I don't like to brag, but even though I've played some pretty terrific rounds of golf in my life, this was the best I have ever played, by far. I must have been inspired from above. My drives were long and true, my irons were accurate and purposeful and my putting was perfect. With all due respect, my play was truly miraculous.'

'There's bad news?' the Pope asked.

Nicklaus sighed. 'I lost to Rabbi Woods by three strokes.'

*   *   *

While playing a round of golf one day, Bill hit a shot into the middle of a field of buttercups. As he was preparing to hit his next shot (probably uprooting most of the buttercups), a voice out of nowhere said: 'Please don't hurt my buttercups.'

Bill, not sure he'd heard correctly, prepared to hit his shot again. Again a voice asked him not to hurt the buttercups.

Bill placed his ball back on the fairway to make his shot and instantly Mother Nature appeared. 'Thank you for not hurting my buttercups. As a reward I will give you a year's supply of butter.'

Bill was momentarily surprised, and then became angry. 'Thanks a lot, lady. But where were you when I was stuck in the pussy willows?!!!'

* * *

A group of golfers go out together for a round and Tom plays brilliantly, finishing three under. The next weekend the foursome goes out again and once more Tom shoots a great round, but the others notice that this week he plays left-handed instead of right. The following two weeks the same story. Left- or right-handed, Tom plays a great game.

Finally one of the others has to ask him: 'How do you decide whether to play left- or right-handed on a particular day?'

The reply is: 'I take a look at which side my wife is sleeping on when I get up and that's the hand I play that day.'

'But what happens if she is on her back?' one player asks.

'I'm a bit late for the game!'

＊　＊　＊

A man was invited to play at his friend's course and during the round felt the call of nature. Far away from the toilets, he went behind a tree believing he was unobserved.

However, three lady members were playing on a parallel fairway. As they passed they were surprised to observe a very private part of a man's anatomy protruding from behind the tree.

'He's certainly not my husband,' said the first lady.

'Disgusting! He's not mine either,' said the second lady.

'It really is a damned cheek,' said the third. 'He's not even a club member!'

＊　＊　＊

A young golfer was playing in his first PGA Tour event. After his practice round he noticed a beautiful young lady by the clubhouse. He went up to her, began talking, and convinced her to come back to his hotel room for the night. All through the night they made wild love together.

In the morning, the woman woke up and arose from bed. The man said: 'Please don't go. I love you and I want you to stay with me.'

The woman replied: 'You don't understand ... I'm a hooker.'

The man said: 'That's no problem. You probably just have too strong a grip.'

☆   ☆   ☆

Jim was sitting on the 19th hole one day looking depressed. The bartender walked up to him and said: 'What's wrong?'

'Well,' Jim replied, 'my golfing buddy of 40 years had a heart attack on the 16th green today.'

'Oh, that must have been really hard on you,' the bartender replied.

'It was,' said Jim. 'It was hit the ball, drag Bob, hit the ball, drag Bob ...'

✫   ✫   ✫

The pro was teaching a young woman how to play and they were working on her grip. After she repeatedly duffed shots, the pro said: 'You have a death-grip on the club and it's killing your power. Just hold the club the same way you would hold your husband's penis.'

The young woman proceeded to hit a drive 200 metres down the middle.

The pro said: 'Great shot! Now, take the club out of your mouth . . .!'

✫   ✫   ✫

They stood at the altar, waiting to be married. The bride-to-be looked down and saw a set of golf clubs beside her groom's feet.

'What on earth are you doing with those golf clubs?' she whispered.

'Well,' he said, 'this won't take all afternoon, will it?'

✱ ✱ ✱

A bloke is driving from Sydney to Melbourne and, noticing that he's getting low on fuel, decides to pull off the freeway and find a service station.

The engine is coughing and spluttering when, thank God, he finds an old-fashioned service station, just near Gundagai. And an old bloke comes out, tugging at his braces.

'Want some petrol?'

'Yeah. Fill 'er up.'

While he's filling the tank, the old bloke looks admiringly at the car.

'What kind of car is this?'

'Well,' said the driver, feeling very proud, 'this is the latest Toyota Lexus.'

'What's it got?'

'Well,' says the driver, 'it's got everything. Power steering, power seats, power sunroof, power mirrors, AM/FM radio with ten-disc CD player in the glove box with 100 watts per channel. Eight-speaker stereo. Rack and pinion steering. Leather interior.

Digital instruments. And a marvellous eight-cylinder engine.'

'Gee,' says the attendant.

'How much for the petrol?'

'That'll be $30.20.'

The driver pulls out his wallet and removes a $20 and a $10 bill. Then he searches his pocket and pulls out a handful of change – and mixed up with the change are some golf tees.

'What are them little wooden things?' asks the old bloke.

'That's what I put my balls on when I drive.'

'Gee,' says the old bloke. 'Them Toyota people think of everything!'

What's the difference between a golfer and a skydiver?

A golfer goes (SMACK) 'Oh no!' A skydiver goes 'Oh no!' (SMACK!)

An elderly couple are playing in the annual club championship. They're in a play-off and all the wife has to do to win is down a 15-centimetre putt. She takes her stance, she misses, they lose the match.

Her husband is ropable. 'I can't believe you missed that putt. It was no longer than my willy!'

She looks over at her husband and smiles sadly. 'Yes, dear, but it was much harder.'

☆　　☆　　☆

A couple of blokes were playing golf together when one was struck by lightning. And he found himself, somewhat singed, standing at the Pearly Gates. St Peter whispered to him that the bolt of lightning had been meant for his golf partner. Considerably miffed, the golfer demanded that he be sent back to earth.

'Well, under the circumstances, that could be arranged,' said St Peter, 'but God doesn't like to admit to mistakes so you'll have to go back to earth as someone else.' And he invited the golfer to devise another identity.

'Okay, I want to go back as a lesbian.'

St Peter was astonished. 'Why a lesbian?'

'That way I can still make love to women – and I can hit from the red tees.'

*   *   *

A bloke takes the day off work and heads for the golf course. He's on the second hole when he notices a frog sitting beside the green. And it's croaking 'Ribbit, nine iron', over and over again.

So he grabs a nine iron and hits the ball to within 25 centimetres of the cup. 'That's amazing! You must be a lucky frog!'

The frog's reply? 'Ribbit. Lucky frog.'

The man picks up the frog and takes it with him to the next hole. 'What do you think, frog?'

'Ribbit, three wood.'

He takes out a three wood and hits a hole in one. By the end of the day, the man has enjoyed the best game of his life and is reluctant to leave the frog. He's just about to pop it in his pocket when the frog says: 'Ribbit. Star City.'

They go to the casino and the bloke asks the frog, 'Now what?'

The frog says: 'Ribbit, roulette.'

They approach the roulette table and the bloke whispers: 'What do you think I should bet?'

The frog replies: 'Ribbit. Three thousand dollars, black six.'

It's a million to one to win but with the frog's track record the bloke piles his chips on black six. And wins a fortune.

Taking his winnings, the man books the best room in the hotel, sits the frog down and says: 'Frog, I don't know how to repay you. You've improved my golf game enormously and won me all this money. I'm very, very grateful.'

The frog looks up at him with big froggy eyes and says: 'Ribbit, kiss me.'

Well, why not? After everything the frog has done it deserves a kiss. Whereupon the frog turns into a beautiful 15-year-old girl.

'And that, Your Honour, is how she ended up in my room.'

✳   ✳   ✳

A priest, a doctor and an engineer were waiting for a particularly slow group of golfers to move on.

The engineer: 'What's with these blokes? We've been waiting for 15 minutes!'

The doctor: 'It's outrageous!'

The priest: 'Here comes the greens keeper. Let's have a word with him.'

So he inquires about the group and their agonisingly slow progress.

The greens keeper: 'They're a group of blind firefighters. They lost their sight while saving our clubhouse when the bushfires swept through last year. So we let them play here any time. Free of charge.'

There is a long silence.

The priest: 'That's so sad. I'll say a special prayer for them tonight.'

The doctor: 'Good idea. And I'm going to contact my ophthalmologist colleagues to see if there's anything that can be done for them.'

The engineer: 'In the meantime, why don't they play at night?'

Why is golf like sex?
Think positive
Bend your knees
Keep your head down
Use your hips
Follow through
Relax

Two blokes were playing a round of golf. One was teeing off at the third hole when a very attractive woman ran past, stark naked. Though somewhat distracted by this event the golfer, showing iron discipline, resumed his stance. As he was about to hit the shot, two men in white coats ran past. He was, naturally, curious but once again took his stance. Whereupon a third man in a white coat went running by, carrying two buckets of sand.

Finally he took his shot. As he was walking down the fairway, he asked his companion what the hell had been going on.

'Well, that lady, once a week, escapes from the mental home beside the course, tears off her clobber and runs across the fairway. The three guys you saw were the nurses. They have a race to see who can catch her first, and the winner gets to carry her back.'

'What about the buckets of sand?'

'Well, he won last week. The buckets of sand are his handicap.'

☆   ☆   ☆

Wife: 'Why don't you play golf with Bob any more?'

Husband: 'Would you continue to play with a bloke who always gets drunk, loses lots of balls, tells lousy jokes while you are putting and generally offends everyone around him on the course?'

Wife: 'Certainly not, dear.'

Husband: 'Well, neither would he.'

* * *

A couple of women were playing golf one sunny Saturday morning. The first of the twosome teed off and watched in horror as her ball headed directly towards a foursome of men playing the next hole. The ball hit one of them, who immediately fell to the ground and rolled around in agony, clasping his hands together at his crotch.

The woman rushed to the man to apologise and explained that she was a physiotherapist. 'And I know I could relieve your pain if you'd allow me.'

'Ummph! Oooh! N-nooo. I'll be all right. I'll be okay in a few minutes.'

But he remained in the foetal position still clasping his hands together at his crotch.

When she persisted he finally allowed her to help him. She gently took his hands away, unzipped his trousers, slipped her hand inside and began to massage him.

'How does that feel?'

'It feels great – but my thumb still hurts like buggery.'

* * *

Four men approached the 16th tee. The first golfer teed off and hooked the ball over a fence, where it hit the front tyre of a passing bus – and was hurled back onto the fairway.

'How on earth did you manage that?'

'Well, you have to know the bus timetable.'

* * *

Two blokes are playing golf when they come upon a couple of ladies playing very slowly. One of the men heads towards them to ask for permission to play through.

He stops about halfway there and returning to his friend, says: 'I can't go up there and talk to them. You wouldn't believe it, but that's my wife and my mistress.'

So his friend says: 'Don't worry, I'll go up and ask them.'

When he's halfway there he turns, comes back and says: 'Small world.'

*　*　*

A bloke is looking for a new caddy. His friend says: 'I know a great one – he's 90 years old but has eyes like a hawk.'

'Okay, tell him I'm playing next week.'

A week later and they head for the green. The golfer slices badly and his ball heads for the rough.

'Caddy, did you see where it went?'

'Yes, I did.'

'Okay then, where is it?'

'I forget.'

*　*　*

A couple whose marriage is in a bit of difficulty see a counsellor. After six appointments there's been little progress. But at the seventh session the counsellor grabs the wife, throws her on his couch and makes love to her.

'There,' he says to the husband, 'that's what she needs every Monday, Wednesday, Saturday and Sunday.'

'Well,' says the husband, 'I could bring her in on Mondays and Wednesdays, but Saturdays and Sundays are my golf days.'

What's the difference between a golf ball and a G-spot?
A bloke will spend 20 minutes looking for a golf ball.

Four international executives are playing a round of golf. On the third hole a beeping sound is heard. The British golfer fumbles in his bag, pulls out a cellular phone, turns away from his partners and has a brief conversation.

'Sorry chaps, but one has to keep one's finger on the pulse.' His companions murmur in agreement.

On the fourth hole there's more beeping. The American says 'Excuse me', places his thumb to his ear and holds his little finger to his mouth. He has an intense conversation before turning back to the bewildered group. 'Oh, it's the latest thing in the US. I've got a microphone grafted into my pinkie and a receiver in my thumb.'

They play a few more holes, at which point there's a loud ringing. The German, who's been leaning over his putt, snaps to attention. 'Ja, ja, ja. Auf Wiedersehen.'

On completing his putt he explains to his partners: 'I have a microphone grafted into my lower lip, and the receiver grafted into my earlobe. To answer the phone all I have to do is straighten my neck.' Everyone is very, very impressed.

Finally, on the 18th hole, muted chimes are heard. The Japanese businessman drops his club, blurts, 'So sorry', and runs into the bushes. Everyone waits.

Fifteen minutes later the American goes to check on his colleague. He finds Mr Tanaka squatting, his trousers around his ankles. His eyes are closed and he's grimacing in pain. 'You okay, Tanaka-san?' he asks. 'Everything is fine,' Mr Tanaka replies. 'Just awaiting fax from Tokyo.'

✫ ✫ ✫

A bloke was playing a round on a quiet day at his local course. Just him, with his wife as caddy. On the seventh hole he slices the ball and it sails over a fence to come to rest near a big old shed. He takes out his nine iron to chip back onto the fairway when his wife says, 'Don't do that, dear. If I open the shed doors on your side and the doors near the fairway, you can see the fairway and play onto the green.'

'Great idea, darling,' he says. And, taking a four iron, proceeds to play his shot through the shed. He takes a tremendous swipe and the ball hits an exposed beam, ricochets and hits his wife on the side of the head. She's dead before she hits the ground.

Months pass and he plays no golf. Finally some mates convince him to come out and make up a four-ball at the local. On the seventh hole he slices yet again, and yet again lands near the old shed. He takes out his nine iron, ready to chip back onto the fairway, when one of his mates stops him. 'No, let me open the shed doors on my side. You do the same and you'll have a clear shot to the green.'

'I can't do that.'

'Why not?'

'Well,' and he speaks in a very, very sad voice, 'something awful happened last time I did that.'

'What was it?'

'I got a seven.'

☆   ☆   ☆

A bloke turns up for golf with his mates and, on the first tee, produces a shocking-pink golf ball.

His mates are incredulous and mocking. Real men don't use pink golf balls.

'But this is no ordinary golf ball,' he explains. 'The colour makes it impossible to lose.'

'Bullshit,' says one of his mates. 'I've been in lots of spots where you'd never see that ball again.'

'Well, in those situations the ball has direction-finding equipment. It emits a loud beep and you just follow the sound until you find it.'

There's a silence while the mates consider this proposition. But one says: 'Okay, smart arse. But what about if you hit it into the water?'

'That's where it really comes into its own. It's got a flotation device that takes it to the surface. Then radio waves sense the nearest bank and solar-powered cells propel it there. You just pick up the ball, dry it in your hankie, and keep playing.'

There's a long silence. 'That's bloody amazing! Where did you get it?'

'I found it.'

☆   ☆   ☆

An Australian professional went to Japan to play in an important tournament. He took his brother as caddy. The first night in Tokyo the golfer had to have an early bedtime but the brother decided to go out on the town. He finished up in a house of ill repute, and upon having had his wicked way with one of the young ladies, heard her scream: 'YAKA-MOTO!! YAKAMOTO!!'

Assured in his mind and ego that this heartfelt cry of 'YAKAMOTO' was an expression of satisfaction at his manhood, the brother/caddy returned to his hotel well satisfied with his night out.

The next day on the course his brother, the pro, is on the difficult 170-metre all-water carry par-three fifth hole.

He pulls out a four iron and drills it as straight as a gun barrel into what he mistakenly thinks is the fifth green. Straight into the hole! The crowd all rise as one and scream 'YAKAMOTO!! YAKAMOTO!!' The caddy brother says to the pro brother: 'I think that means it was a great shot.'

To which the more experienced pro brother replies: 'No, actually YAKAMOTO in Japanese means "wrong hole".'

✳   ✳   ✳

A puzzled golfer watched a fellow member don some very unorthodox gear in the clubroom. 'How long have you been wearing a brassiere?' he asked.

'Ever since my wife found it in the car.'

* * *

A golfer is just starting out on the tour. During his first match, in which he is going well, he spots a beautiful woman watching his every move. He thinks to himself: 'If I play my cards right I could take her back to the motel.'

He successfully woos her back to his room, where they make love. When he finishes, he gets out of bed and she says: 'Where are you going?' He says: 'I'm going to ring up room service and get a bottle of champagne.' She says: 'Jack Nicklaus would never leave a girl after he's made love to her once – get back into bed.'

So they go for it a second time. When he's finished, he gets out of bed. 'Where are you going?' she asks. 'I'm going to ring up room service and get a bottle of champagne,' he says. She says: 'Jack Nicklaus would never leave a girl after he's made love to her twice – back into bed!' So they saddle up for the third time.

When he gets out of bed, she asks: 'Well, I

suppose you're ringing up room service to get a bottle of champagne?'

He says: 'No, I'm ringing up Jack Nicklaus to find out the par for this hole!!'

Mildred, shut up,' cried the golfer at his nagging wife. 'Shut up or you'll drive me out of my mind.'

'That,' said Mildred, 'wouldn't be a drive. It would be a short putt.'

A young American golf fanatic six months new to the game decided to make the trip of a lifetime to Scotland, the Holy Land of golf. Upon his arrival he quickly headed out to the course and arranged a tee-time for a short time later. As per his PGA teaching professional's instructions, he requested and secured the best caddy the course had to offer: Olde Angus, the pride of the links for 53 years.

Happily the young American set off on his dream round, but 15 holes later, numb and disgusted, 43 strokes over par, he reached over, grabbed his clubs and bag from Olde Angus and tossed them over the cliff into the churning sea below.

Turning to Angus, and with the spittle of frustration coming from his mouth, he said: 'Angus, you are positively the worst caddy on the face of the earth.' To which Olde Angus replied: 'Nay, I dunna think that's possible, laddie. It would be far too much of a coincidence.'

☆   ☆   ☆

My friend,' said St Peter to the recently deceased, 'you did lead an exemplary life on earth. But there is one instance of your taking the name of the Lord in vain. Would you care to tell us about it?'

'I recall,' replied the new applicant, 'it was in 1965 on the last hole at Pinehurst. I only needed a par four to break 70 for the first time in my life.'

'Was your drive good?' asked St Peter, with increasing interest.

'Right down the middle. But when I got to my ball, it was plugged deep in a wet rut made by a drunk's golf car.'

'Oh dear,' said St Peter. 'A real sucker! Is that when you ...'

'No, I'm pretty good with a three iron. I played the ball close to my feet, caught the sweet spot and moved it right onto the green. But it bounced on a twig or something – it was a very windy day – and slid off the apron right under the steepest lip of the trap.'

'What a pity!' said St Peter consolingly. 'Then that must have been when ...'

'No, I gritted my teeth, dug in with an open stance, swung a smooth outside arc, and back-spun a bucket's worth of sand up onto the green. When everything settled down, there was my ball, only 25 centimetres off the cup.'

'JESUS CHRIST!' shrieked St Peter. 'Don't tell me you missed the bloody putt!'

For James it was a masterly addressing of the ball, a magnificent swing, but somehow, something went wrong and a horrible slice resulted. The ball went onto the adjoining fairway and hit a man full force. He dropped.

James and his partner ran up to the stricken victim, who lay, quite unconscious, with the ball between his feet.

'Good heavens!' exclaimed James. 'What shall I do?'

'Don't move him,' said his partner. 'If we leave him here he becomes an immovable obstruction and you can either play the ball as it lies or drop it two club lengths away.'

Man playing by himself on a gorgeous clear morning, thinking he wouldn't be dead for quids. After parring the first two holes, he lines up on the third, a 400-metre par four, and hits a screamer down the middle. He lines up his second with a three iron, but shanks it. It hits a tree, ricochets

back and hits him between the eyes, and he drops
dead on the fairway.

His spirit floats up to the Pearly Gates. 'Who
are you?' says St Peter.

'Bill Anderson,' says Bill Anderson.

St Peter looks at his clipboard and scratches his
head. 'I've got no record of your being due; what
are you here for?'

'Two.'

✯   ✯   ✯

A man came running into the clubhouse and asked
if there was a doctor available.

'Yes,' replied one man, 'I'm a doctor. What's
wrong?'

The man, still short of breath, said, 'My female
playing partner has been hit by a ball and is out
cold on the fairway.'

'Where was she hit?' asked the doctor.

'Between the first and second holes,' replied the
man.

'Bloody hell!' replied the doctor. 'Doesn't leave
much room for a bandaid.'

HAIL TO THE CHIEF

HEAVEN'S GATE

HIGH FINANCE

HIGHER EDUCATION

HORIZONTAL TANGO

HAIL TO THE CHIEF

Hillary phones Bill and says: 'Honey, I'm pregnant.' There's a brief silence and Bill says: 'Who's calling?'

* * *

Bill Clinton, Al Gore and Bill Gates were flying from Washington to Los Angeles in Bill Gates's jet when it crashed into the Rockies. They found themselves in heaven, with God sitting on a great white throne. God spoke to Al first. 'Al, what do you believe in?'

'Well, I believe that the combustion engine is evil,' replied Gore, 'and that we need to save the world from CFCs and that if any more freon is used the earth will become a greenhouse and we'll all die.'

God said: 'Fine, fine, I can live with that. Come and sit on my left.'

God then turned his attention to the President. 'Bill, what do you believe in?'

Bill replied: 'Well, I believe in power to the people. I think people should be able to make their own choices about things and that no one should ever be able to tell someone else what to do. I also believe in feeling people's pain.'

'Okay, that sounds good,' said God. 'Come and sit on my right.'

God then addressed Bill Gates. 'Bill, what do you believe?'

And Bill said: 'I believe you're in my chair.'

What does Bill say to Hillary after sex?
I'll be home in 20 minutes.

Did you hear about the new White House soup?
It's a little weenie in a lot of hot water.

Why did Bill Clinton stop playing the saxophone?
He was too busy playing the hormonica.

A hundred women were surveyed: 'Would you have sex with Bill Clinton?' Eighty per cent said 'Not again'.

How will everyone remember Bill Clinton in history?
The president after Bush.

What's the game they're playing in the White House?
Swallow the leader.

Bill Clinton went to Baghdad to negotiate peace with Saddam Hussein. On sitting down in the conference room the President noted Hussein had three buttons on the arm of his chair. After a few minutes Hussein pressed the first button and a boxing glove appeared and hit Clinton square on the jaw. In the spirit of peace Clinton decided to ignore this and continued negotiating, until Hussein pressed the second button – and a wooden bat swung out and clobbered Bill on the noggin. Saddam started laughing uproariously, but once again, Bill ignored the provocation. A moment later Clinton saw Saddam press the third button and a big leather boot sprang out and kicked him in the balls. Deciding he'd had enough, Clinton returned to Washington.

Three weeks later the negotiations were re-scheduled at the White House, and as Hussein sat down in Bill's conference he noticed the President had, yes, three buttons on the arm of *his* chair. A few seconds later, Bill pressed the first button but nothing seemed to happen. Nonetheless the President started giggling. Then he pressed the second button – and, flinching, Hussein waited for the worst. But once again, nothing happened. Yet the President was laughing even louder. A few minutes later Clinton pressed the third button and almost fell out of his chair, he was laughing so uproariously. But why? Nothing had happened!

Nonetheless Hussein had had enough. He stood

up and said: 'That's it! I'm going back to Baghdad.'
To which Clinton replied: 'What Baghdad?'

Dan Quayle, Newt Gingrich and Bill Clinton are travelling in a car in the mid-west. A tornado comes along and whirls them up into the air, tossing them thousands of metres away. When they come down and extract themselves from the vehicle, they realise they're in the Land of Oz. Quayle says: 'I'm going to ask the wizard for a brain.' Gingrich says: 'I'm going to ask the wizard for a heart.'

And Clinton says: 'Where's Dorothy?'

How did Bill and Hillary meet?
They were dating the same girl in school.

What does the band play when Clinton enters the room?
'Kneel to the Chief'.

Why does Bill Clinton wear underwear?
To keep his ankles warm.

Why does Hillary want to have sex with Bill first thing in the morning?
She wants to be first lady.

What did Bill Clinton say when asked if he had used protection?
'Sure, there was a guard sitting right outside the door.'

☆   ☆   ☆

It is winter at the White House and the rose garden is covered in snow. Clinton is strolling in the precinct when he notices the word 'Bastard' written in golden piss. Outraged, he goes into the Oval Office and calls the CIA and FBI to find out the author of this insult. When they return they say: 'Mr President, we've got bad news and we've got worse news. Which would you like first?'

And the President says: 'What's the bad news?'
The agents say: 'It was Al Gore.'

Aghast, the President yells: 'That dirty, no-good son of a bitch! What's the worse news?'

And the agents chorus: 'It was in Hillary's handwriting.'

The President invited Jerry Falwell to fly across country on *Air Force One*. The flight attendant came around for drink orders. The President asked for his usual glass of bourbon, but Falwell was outraged at the offer of alcohol. 'I'd rather be savagely raped by a brazen whore,' he told the purser, 'than let liquor touch these lips.' Whereupon the President handed back his bourbon and said: 'I didn't know there was a choice. I'll have what he's having.'

Two young interns are hired at the White House. They're walking down the hall when President Clinton sees them. He walks up and says: 'Gee, I've never come across your faces before.'

President Clinton walks around the White House all day with a pair of pink ladies' panties on his arm. He even wears them to meetings of Cabinet. Reporters and staff observe the phenomenon and wonder what he is doing.

At an afternoon press conference a reporter gets brave enough to ask him. 'Sir, why do you have a pair of ladies' pants on your arm?'

The President replies: 'It's a patch. I'm trying to quit.'

One Sunday morning, Chelsea burst into the living quarters of the White House and said: 'Dad, Mom, I have some great news for you. I'm getting married to the biggest hunk at Stanford. He lives in Palo Alto and his name is Dennis.'

After dinner, the President took Chelsea aside: 'Honey, I have to talk with you. Your mother and I have been married a long time. She's a wonderful wife but she's never offered much excitement in the bedroom, so I used to fool around with women a lot. Dennis is actually your half-brother, and I'm afraid you can't marry him.'

Chelsea was heartbroken. After eight months she eventually started dating again. A year later she came home and very proudly announced: 'Robert asked me to marry him! We're getting married in June.'

Again her father insisted on a private conversation and broke the sad news. 'Robert is your half-brother too,' honey. I'm awfully sorry about this.'

Chelsea was furious! She finally decided to go to her mother with the news. 'Dad has done so much harm. I guess I'm never going to get married,' she complained. 'Every time I fall in love, Dad tells me the guy is my half-brother.'

Hillary just shook her head. 'Don't pay any attention to what he says, dear. He's not really your father.'

Saddam Hussein called President Clinton and said: 'Bill, I called you because I had this incredible dream last night. I could see all of America, and it was beautiful and on top of every building there was a flag.'

Clinton asked: 'Saddam, what was on the flag?'

Saddam responded: 'It said Allah is God, God is Allah.'

Clinton said: 'You know, Saddam, I'm really glad you called, because last night I had a dream too. I could see all of Baghdad, and it was even more beautiful than before the war. It had been completely rebuilt, and on every building there was a flag.'

Saddam said: 'Bill, what was on the flag?'

Clinton replied: 'I really don't know, Saddam ... I don't read Hebrew!'

What does Bill Clinton have in common with former great presidents?
Nothing.

What is the difference between a liberal and a puppy?
A puppy stops whining after it grows up.

Why aren't Clinton White House staffers given coffee breaks?
It takes too long to retrain them.

What were the three toughest years in Bill Clinton's life?
Grade 6.

If you had Bill Clinton, Al Gore and Dolly Parton on stage together, what would you have?
Two boobs and a great country singer.

Why are females of the White House staff furious at Hillary?
She keeps leaving the toilet seat up.

Bill, Hillary and Al are in a boat. The boat sinks. Who is saved?
The United States of America.

Why is Chelsea growing up a confused child?
Because Dad can't keep his pants on and Mum wants to wear them.

What does Teddy Kennedy have that Bill Clinton wishes *he* did?
A dead girlfriend.

Did you hear Chrysler is introducing a new car to commemorate President Clinton's reign?
It's going to be called the Dodge Drafter.

Why does the secret service guard Hillary so closely?
Because if something happens to her, Bill becomes President.

How many Bill Clintons does it take to change a light bulb?
None – he'll only promise to change it.

How is Bill Clinton like John McEnroe?
They both say it was out, but the judges say it was in.

What's the difference between Monica's blue dress and Bill Clinton?
The blue dress will eventually come clean.

A right-wing spin doctor who'd spun
Lurid tales about Monica's fun
Exclaimed when his eyes
Saw the fruit of his lies
'We've gotten O.J. off page one!'

Said a president thought to give pecks
To areas other than necks
'Although it's most sultry
it isn't adultery
I'm not even sure that it's sex.'

There once was a woman named Monica
Bill met her on the first day of Hanukkah
She wore a beret
Didn't have much to say
But man, could she play the harmonica!

Bill Clinton meets Ken Starr sitting on a park bench in Washington. Clinton sits down and, after a while, asks Starr: 'Have you been getting any on the side lately?' A surprised Starr responds: 'You know, Bill ... it's been so long since I've had any, I didn't know they moved it.'

Similarities Between Nixon and Clinton

Nixon: Tricky Dick.
Clinton: Licky Dick.

Nixon: Watergate.
Clinton: Waterbed.

Nixon: His biggest fear – the Cold War.
Clinton: His biggest fear – a cold sore.

Nixon: Brought down by Deep Throat.
Clinton: Brought down by Deep Throat.

Nixon: Deep Throat leaked to the press.
Clinton: Deep Throat leaked on her dress.

Nixon: Worried about carpet bombs.
Clinton: Worried about carpet burns.

Nixon: His Vice-President was a Greek.
Clinton: His Vice-President is a geek.

Nixon: Couldn't stop Kissinger.
Clinton: Couldn't stop kissing her.

Nixon: Ex-president.
Clinton: Sex-president.

Nixon: Well acquainted with G. Gordon Liddy.
Clinton: Well acquainted with the G-spot.

✷   ✷   ✷

Blow jobs and land deals in backwater places
Big Macs and french fries and girls with big faces
Lots of nice cleavage that makes Willie spring
These are a few of my favourite things.

Susan McDougal and Gennifer Flowers
Horny young interns who while 'way the hours
Profits from futures that Hillary brings
These are a few of my favourite things.

Beating the draft board and getting elected
Naming to judgeships some hacks I've selected
Conspiracy theories that blame the right wing
These are a few of my favourite things.

Golfing with Vernon and suborning perjury
Falling down drunk that required knee surgery
Stars in the White House who come here to sing
These are a few of my favourite things.

Meeting with Boris and Helmut and Tony
States of the Union with lots of boloney
Winning debates and the joy of my flings
These are a few of my favourite things.

(chorus)
When Miss Jones bites
When Ken Starr stings
When I'm feeling sad
I simply remember my favourite things
And then I don't feel ... so bad.

☆　　☆　　☆

A guy walks into a bar and asks for a beer. When he sits down, he notices that Clinton is giving a speech on the TV. He turns to the guy on his right and says: 'Bill Clinton is such a horse's arse.' The guy punches him right in the face and knocks him off his stool onto the floor.

The first guy gets back up off the floor and sees Hillary on the screen. He turns to the guy on his left and says: 'Hillary Clinton is such a horse's arse.' That guy also punches him in the face and knocks him off his stool onto the floor.

When the first guy gets back up on his stool, he motions for the barman to come over and whispers to him: 'This must really be Clinton Country!' The barman answers, 'No, it's not ... it's horse country.'

Monica walks into her dry-cleaning store and tells the guy: 'I've got another dress for you to clean.'

Slightly hard of hearing, the clerk says: 'Come again?'

'No,' says Monica, 'mustard.'

President Clinton's going to change the US national anthem to 'Yank on my doodle, it's a dandy'.

*T*itanic video: $9.99 on Internet.
Clinton video: $9.99 on Internet.

Titanic video: Over three hours long.
Clinton video: Over three hours long.

Titanic video: The story of Jack and Rose, their forbidden love and a subsequent catastrophe.
Clinton video: The story of Bill and Monica, their forbidden love and a subsequent catastrophe.

Titanic video: Celine Dion sings 'My Heart Will Go On'.
Clinton video: Bill Clinton thinks 'My Hard Will Go On'.

Titanic video: Jack is a starving artist.
Clinton video: Bill is a bullshit artist.

Titanic video: In one part, Jack enjoys a good cigar.
Clinton video: In one part, Bill enjoys a good cigar.

Titanic video: During the ordeal, Rose's dress gets ruined.
Clinton video: During the ordeal, Monica's dress gets ruined.

Titanic video: Rose undresses and exposes her breasts.
Clinton video: Monica undresses and exposes her breasts.

Titanic video: Jack teaches Rose to spit.
Clinton video: Bill ... never mind.

Titanic video: Rose gets to keep her jewellery.
Clinton video: Monica is forced to return her gifts.

Titanic video: Not enough lifeboats.
Clinton video: Not enough lifeboats.

Titanic aftermath: Leonardo DiCaprio is wildly popular.
Clinton aftermath: Bill Clinton is wildly popular.

Titanic finale: Jack meets an icy death.
Clinton finale: Bill goes home to Hillary.

Dear John Hinkley,

Ronnie and I are concerned about your wellbeing. We also wanted to write and assure you that we have no bitterness towards you. We all make mistakes in life and you are no different. It is important that we learn from them. Once again, we wish you good health and speedy recovery and hope to see you as a responsible, functioning adult in the world outside of prison.

All our best,

Ronald and Nancy Reagan

P.S. We both thought you would like to know that Bill Clinton is sleeping with Jodie Foster.

Bill and Hillary were married for 40 years. When they first got married, Bill said: 'I'm putting a box under the bed. You must promise never to look in it.' In all their 40 years of marriage Hillary never looked.

However, on the afternoon of their 40th anniversary, curiosity got the best of her and she lifted the lid and peeked inside. In the box were three empty beer cans and $1874.25 in cash. She closed the box and put it back under the bed. Now that she knew what was in the box, she was doubly curious as to why. That evening they went out for a special dinner.

After dinner, Hillary could no longer contain her curiosity and confessed, saying: 'I am so sorry.

For all these years I kept my promise and never looked into the box under our bed. However, today the temptation was too much and I gave in. But now I need to know why you keep those cans in the box.'

Bill said, 'I guess after all these years you deserve to know the truth. Whenever I was unfaithful to you I put an empty beer can in the box under the bed to remind myself not to do it again.'

Hillary was shocked, but said: 'I am very disappointed and saddened but I guess that after all those years away from home on the road, temptation does happen.' And she thought to herself, 'I guess three times is not that bad considering the years.'

They hugged and made their peace. A little while later Hillary asked Bill: 'Why do you have all that money in the box?'

Bill answered: 'Whenever the box filled with empties, I cashed them in.'

One night, Bill Clinton was awakened by George Washington's ghost in the White House. Clinton saw him and asked: 'George, what is the best thing I could do to help the country?'

'Set an honest and honourable example, just as I did,' advised George.

The next night, the ghost of Thomas Jefferson moved through the dark bedroom. 'Tom, what is the best thing I could do to help the country?' Clinton asked.

'Cut taxes and reduce the size of government,' advised Tom.

Clinton didn't sleep well the next night, and saw another figure moving in the shadows. It was Abraham Lincoln's ghost. 'Abe, what is the best thing I could do to help the country?' Clinton asked.

'Go to the theatre.'

HEAVEN'S GATE

Two blokes are checking into heaven. They compare notes on their deaths.

'I froze to death,' says one.

The other explains that, suspicious of his wife, he arranged to get home early and as he opened the door could smell an unfamiliar cologne. He searched the house for a sexual trespasser while his wife proclaimed her innocence at the top of her voice. 'I couldn't find a lover, but finally, in a wrestling match with the missus, toppled off a balcony.'

'It's a pity you didn't look in the freezer,' said the other, as St Peter stamped his passport. 'Then both of us would be alive today.'

✶   ✶   ✶

A gold prospector falls down a forgotten mineshaft at Wedderburn and wakes up dead. Dusting himself down, he looks up to see the shimmering loveliness of heaven's gates but he's concerned that St Peter is shaking his head.

'Sorry, nothing personal. But there's absolutely no room in heaven for another gold prospector. We've got our quota.'

The prospector is momentarily nonplussed. Then he gets an idea. He yells out: 'GOLD DISCOVERED IN HELL!'

Whereupon some hundreds of prospectors rush through the Pearly Gates and head south.

'Very ingenious,' says St Peter admiringly. 'You may now enter.'

'No thanks,' says the prospector, already heading in the opposite direction.

'Where the hell are you going?' asks St Peter.

'Down there. After all, there might be some truth in the rumour.'

★　★　★

Three blondes die and are at the Pearly Gates of heaven. St Peter tells them that they can enter the gates if they can answer one simple question.

St Peter asks the first blonde: 'What is Easter?'

The blonde replies: 'Oh, that's easy! It's the holiday in November when everyone gets together, eats turkey, and is thankful . . .'

'Wrong!' replies St Peter, and proceeds to ask the second blonde the same question. 'What is Easter?'

The second blonde replies: 'Easter is the holiday in December when you put up a nice tree, exchange presents and celebrate the birth of Jesus.'

St Peter looks at the second blonde, shakes his head in disgust, and tells her she's wrong too.

He then peers over his glasses at the third blonde and asks: 'What is Easter?'

The third blonde smiles confidently and looks St Peter in the eyes: 'I know what Easter is.'

'Oh?' says St Peter incredulously.

'Easter is the Christian holiday that coincides with the Jewish celebration of Passover. Jesus and his disciples were eating at the last supper and

Jesus was later deceived and turned over to the Romans by one of his disciples. The Romans took him to be crucified and he was stabbed in the side, made to wear a crown of thorns, and was hung on a cross with nails through his hands. He was buried in a nearby cave which was sealed off by a large boulder.'

St Peter smiles broadly with delight. The third blonde continues: 'Every year the boulder is moved aside so that Jesus can come out, and if he sees his shadow, there will be six more weeks of winter.'

☆　☆　☆

After dying, a cat walks up to the Pearly Gates where he meets St Peter. St Peter says to the cat: 'During your time on earth you were a good little cat. You kept your master's house and shed free of pests, and for this faithful service, you get one wish for anything you would particularly like.'

The cat thinks for a moment before replying: 'Well, my master had a satin pillow that I loved, so I would like a satin pillow just like that one.'

St Peter replies: 'Go on through, you'll find it waiting.'

A little while later a group of fieldmice appear at the Pearly Gates. St Peter greets them, saying: 'During your time on earth you were good little fieldmice. You kept the other pests from destroying the farmer's crop, so as a reward you may have anything you like in heaven.'

The fieldmice converse briefly before one steps forward and says: 'The farmer's children had roller skates, and they looked like a lot of fun, so that's what we'd like.'

St Peter replies: 'Go on through, you'll find them waiting.'

A while later St Peter is strolling through heaven when he comes across the cat, who is sitting on his satin pillow purring contentedly. 'So, how are you enjoying heaven?' St Peter inquires.

'Oh, it's wonderful,' answers the cat. 'This pillow is just divine, even better than the one I had on earth, and the Meals on Wheels,' he kisses his paw, 'nice touch!'

* * *

Everybody on earth dies and goes to heaven. God comes and says: 'I want the men to make two lines. One line for the men that dominated their women on earth, and the other line for the men that were dominated by their women. Also, I want all the women to go with St Peter.'

With that said and done, the next time God looks the women are gone and there are two lines. The line of the men that were dominated by their women is 100 kilometres long, and the line of men that dominated their women has only one man in it.

God gets mad and says: 'You men should be ashamed of yourselves. I created you in my image and you were all whipped by your mates. Look at the only one of my sons who stood up and made me proud. Learn from him! Tell them, my son, how did you manage to be the only one in this line?'

And the man replies: 'I don't know, my wife told me to stand here.'

✶ ✶ ✶

A teacher, a garbage collector and a lawyer arrived at the Pearly Gates simultaneously. St Peter informed them that in order to get into heaven they'd each have to answer a question, but it wouldn't be difficult. You wouldn't need to have a PhD in Ancient Greek. In fact, he found that people liked questions about the movies. So he said to the teacher: 'What was the name of the great big ship that crashed into the iceberg?'

The teacher said: *'Titanic! Titanic!'* And St Peter let him through the gate.

Then he turned to the garbage man. 'And how many people died on the ship?'

'Fifteen hundred,' came the answer, without a moment's hesitation.

It was the lawyer's turn. 'Now give me their names, their addresses, their dates of birth, the names of their parents, the names of their children ...'

HIGH FINANCE

An American businessman was at the pier of a small coastal Mexican village when a little boat with just one fisherman docked. Inside the boat were several large yellowfin tuna.

The American complimented the Mexican on the quality of his fish and asked how long it took to catch them.

The Mexican replied: 'Only a little while.'

The American then asked why he didn't stay out longer and catch more fish.

The Mexican said he had enough to support his family's immediate needs.

The American then asked: 'But what do you do with the rest of your time?'

The Mexican fisherman said: 'I sleep late, fish a little, play with my children, take siesta with my wife Maria, stroll into the village each evening where

I sip wine and play guitar with my amigos. I have a full and busy life, Señor.'

The American scoffed. 'I am a Harvard MBA and could help you. You should spend more time fishing and with the proceeds, buy a bigger boat. With the proceeds from the bigger boat you could buy several boats. Eventually you would have a fleet of fishing boats. Instead of selling your catch to a middleman, you would sell directly to the processor, eventually opening your own cannery. You would control the product, processing and distribution. You would need to leave this small coastal fishing village and move to Mexico City, then LA and eventually NYC where you would run your expanding enterprise.'

The Mexican fisherman asked: 'But Señor, how long would this all take?'

To which the American replied: 'Fifteen to 20 years.'

'But what then, Señor?'

The American laughed and said: 'That's the best part. When the time is right you would announce a management buyout, then have a public float, become very rich and sell your company stock to the public. You would make millions.'

'Millions, Señor? Then what?'

The American said: 'Then you would retire. Move to a small coastal fishing village where you would sleep late, fish a little, play with your kids, take siesta with your wife, stroll to the village in the evening where you could sip wine and play guitar with your amigos.'

HIGHER EDUCATION

A linguistics professor was lecturing to his class one day. 'In English,' he said, 'a double negative forms a positive. In some languages, though, such as Russian, a double negative is still a negative. However, there is no language where a double positive can form a negative.'

A voice from the back of the room piped up: 'Yeah, right.'

* * *

There was a maths class and the teacher picked a youngster in the middle of the class to answer a question.

'If there were five birds sitting on a fence and you shot one with a gun, how many would be left?'

'None,' said the child, 'cos the rest would fly away.'

'The real answer is four,' said the teacher, 'but I like the way you were thinking.'

'Then I've got a question for you,' said the child. 'If there were three women eating ice-cream cones in a milk bar and one was licking her cone, the second was biting her cone and the third was sucking the cone, which one is married?'

'Well ...' said the teacher nervously, 'the one sucking the cone?'

'No,' said the boy, 'the one with the wedding ring on her finger. But I like the way you were thinking.'

＊　＊　＊

You Know You've Been Out of Uni Too Long When ...

Your pot plants stay alive.
Having sex in a single bed is absurd.
You keep more food than beer in the fridge.

Six a.m. is when you get up, not when you go to sleep.

You hear your favourite song in the lift at work.

You carry an umbrella.

Your friends marry and divorce instead of getting together and breaking up.

You go from 130 days of holidays to seven.

Jeans and a jumper no longer qualify as 'dressed up'.

You're the one calling the police because those damn kids next door don't know how to turn down the stereo.

You don't know what time the pizza joint closes any more.

Your car insurance goes down and your car payments go up.

Sleeping on the couch is a no-no.

You no longer take naps from noon to 6 p.m.

Dinner and a movie – the whole date instead of the beginning of one.

You go to the chemist for Panadol and antacids, not condoms and pregnancy test kits.

A $6 bottle of wine is no longer 'pretty good stuff'.
You actually eat breakfast foods at breakfast time.
Grocery lists are longer than: Macaroni and Cheese,
Diet Coke, CCs.
'I just can't drink the way I used to' replaces 'I'm
never going to drink that much again'.
Over 90 per cent of the time you spend in front of
a computer is for real work.

HORIZONTAL TANGO

A bloke picks up a woman at a pub and they book into a motel. He starts performing cunnilingus and, from time to time, lifts his head and makes a remark about the *Lusitania*. 'Its sinking came as a complete shock. The world was horrified.'

Then he returns to his task, only to lift his head up again. 'Twelve hundred lives were lost.'

And he returns to his task. 'But it forced the US into the war.'

Finally the woman has had enough of this. 'Where are you getting all this crap about the *Lusitania*?'

'From the bit of paper stuck to your bum.'

☆　☆　☆

A woman was in bed with her lover when she

heard her husband opening the front door. 'Hurry!' she said. 'Stand in the corner.' She quickly rubbed baby oil all over him and then dusted him with talcum powder. 'Don't move until I tell you to,' she whispered. 'Just pretend you're a statue.'

'What's this, honey?' the husband inquired as he entered the room.

'Oh, it's just a statue,' she replied nonchalantly. 'The Smiths bought one for their bedroom. I liked it so much, I got one for us, too.'

No more was said about the statue, not even later that night when they went to sleep.

Around 2.00 in the morning the husband got out of bed, went to the kitchen and returned a while later with a sandwich and a glass of milk.

'Here,' he said to the 'statue'. 'Eat something. I stood like an idiot at the Smiths' for three days, and nobody offered me so much as a glass of water.'

☆　　☆　　☆

A man and a woman who've never met before find themselves in the same sleeping compartment on an interstate train. After initial embarrassment they do their best to ignore each other and prepare for sleep, the woman on the top bunk, the man on the lower.

After a few minutes the woman leans over and says: 'I'm sorry to bother you, but I'm awfully cold. I was wondering if you could possibly pass me another blanket.'

The man looks up with a glint in his eye and says: 'I've got a better idea ... Let's pretend we're married.'

'Why not?' giggles the woman.

'Good,' he says. 'Get your own fucking blanket!'

Three women get together for coffee and the topic of conversation turns to contraception.

The first woman says: 'We've used the rhythm method for years. The Holy Father approves of it and it's surprisingly effective – it's only ever failed us twice.'

The second woman says: 'We don't go for all

that pious claptrap. We've always used the Pill. It's easy. It doesn't rob us of our pleasure and it's only ever failed us once.'

The third woman says: 'We've always used the plate-and-bucket method. My husband and I met in the army and it was hard to get any private time with each other, so we'd usually hide out in a closet somewhere. My husband, being shorter than me, would have to stand on a bucket. When I'd see his eyes get as big and round as plates I'd kick the bucket out from under him. It's never failed.'

☆   ☆   ☆

A bloke goes to his doctor to complain that his wife hasn't had sex with him for the last seven months. The doctor suggests that his wife make an appointment.

'And why don't you want to have sex with your husband any more?' he asks when she visits the surgery.

'For the last seven months I've taken a cab to work every morning. But I don't have any money.

So the cab driver asks me "So you're going to pay me today? Or what?" So it's "Or what". Which makes me late for work. And the boss asks me "So are we going to take 20 bucks from your pay? Or what?" So it's another "Or what". And when I go home at night the cab driver says "So you're going to pay me this time? Or what?" So it's "Or what" again. So you see, doctor, I'm all tired out. And I don't want it any more.'

The doctor looks at her very, very seriously. 'So are we going to tell your husband? Or what?'

*　　*　　*

A lawyer married a woman who'd had a number of previous husbands. On their wedding night the bride said to her new groom: 'Please promise to be gentle ... I'm a virgin.'

This puzzled the groom considerably. He asked his new bride to explain.

'Well, my first husband was a teacher. And he said "Those who can, do, those who can't, teach".

'My next husband was an engineer. He told me

he understood the basic process but needed three years to research, implement and design a new method.

'My next husband was a psychiatrist and all he ever wanted to do was talk about it.

'My next was a gynaecologist and all he ever wanted to do was look at it.

'My twelfth husband? He was a stamp collector and all he ever wanted to do was ... God, I miss him!

'So now I've married you, a lawyer. And I know I'm really going to get screwed.'

A bloke applied to join a nudist club.

'What exactly do you do here?' he asked.

'It's very simple,' said the club secretary. 'We take off all our clothes and commune with nature.'

'Great,' said the bloke, so he handed over his Amex, took off his gear and went for a walk.

As he strolled down a path he saw a large sign reading: BEWARE OF GAYS.

A little further along he saw a second sign. It was identical: BEWARE OF GAYS.

He continued walking until he came to a small clearing which had a small bronze plaque set in the ground. And he had to bend right over to read the tiny lettering. It said: 'Sorry, but you had two warnings!'

He: 'Have I shown you my magic watch?'
She: 'No, what does it do?'
He: 'It tells me that you're not wearing any knickers.'
She: 'Well, your watch is fucked, because I am.'
He: 'Damn, it must be an hour fast.'

A man and a woman were having a drink, getting to know one another, and started bantering back and forth about male/female issues. They talked about who was better in certain sports, who were the better entertainers, etc. The flirting continued for more than an hour when the topic of sex came up. So they got into an argument about who enjoyed sex more.

The man said: 'Men obviously enjoy sex more than women. Why do you think we're so obsessed with getting laid?'

He then went on for several hours arguing his point, even going so far as to ask other men in the pub for their opinions. The woman listened quietly until the man was finished making his point. Confident in the strength of his argument, the man awaited her response.

'That doesn't prove anything,' the woman countered. 'Think about this: when your ear itches and you put your little finger in it and wiggle it around, then pull it out, which feels better – your ear or your finger?'

* * *

The general was dictating to his new secretary. She noticed his fly was open and said: 'Sir, your barracks door is open.'

Looking down, he saw that his zipper was undone and hastened to get his uniform in order.

It was a moot point which of the two was the more embarrassed.

'I'm sorry about the barracks door. And I hope you didn't see a soldier standing at attention.'

'No sir. Just a little disabled veteran sitting on two duffle bags.'

☆　　☆　　☆

It was a wet night in Sydney. A taxi driver spotted an arm waving from the shadows and, even before he rolled to a stop, a figure leapt into the cab and slammed the door. Checking his rear-vision mirror he was startled to see that his passenger was a dripping wet and completely naked woman.

'Where to, Miss?' he stammered.

'Kings Cross,' she replied.

'Fine, fine,' he said, taking another long look in the mirror.

'Just what the hell do you think you're looking at, driver?'

'Well,' he answered, 'I couldn't help but wonder how you'll pay your fare.'

Whereupon the woman put her feet up on the front seat, smiled at the driver and said: 'Does this answer your question?'

Still looking in the mirror, the cabbie said: 'Got anything smaller?'

The bloke was upset when his girlfriend broke off their engagement and asked for her photograph back.

So he went and collected photographs of women from his friends, bundled them together, and sent them to her with a note: 'Regret cannot remember which one is you. Please keep your photo and return the others.'

A truckie asks his wife: 'Why don't you ever tell me when you're having an orgasm?'

She replies: 'Because you're never there.'

A bloke goes to a prostitute in Kings Cross. He asks: 'How much?'

She says: 'Fifty dollars.'

'But I've only got $10.'

'Okay.'

A couple of days later the guy discovers the worst. So he goes to the prostitute and says: 'You bloody well gave me crabs!'

And she says: 'Well what the fuck do you expect for $10 – lobster?'

A couple have recently hit upon hard times. One night the husband comes home and says to his wife: 'Darling, you know money is a bit tight at the moment, so I've been thinking. I have got a few ideas as to how we can reduce our outlays and get over the current hard times. Firstly, you could learn to cook. Maybe just two or three evening meals and we would save the money that we spend on going out to dinner. I'm sure it wouldn't be too difficult. Perhaps you could also start to run the vacuum cleaner around the house and dust once a week, and that way we wouldn't need the services of the house cleaner. That's bound to save some money. Thirdly, you could learn to do some washing and ironing. It's not much to ask. Just five shirts on a Sunday night and we wouldn't need to send them to the laundry. That would save a bit more money. So, darling, do you have any thoughts?'

'Well,' the wife responded. 'Maybe you could learn to fuck and then we could get rid of the gardener.'

* * *

Jane met Tarzan in the jungle. She was very attracted to him and during her questions about his life she asked him how he managed for sex. 'What's that?' he asked. She explained to him what sex was and he said, 'Oh, I use a hole in the trunk of a tree.'

Horrified, she said, 'Tarzan, you have it all wrong. I'll show you how to do it properly.' She took off her clothes, lay down on the ground and spread her legs wide. 'Here,' she said, 'you must put it in here.'

Tarzan removed his loincloth, stepped closer and then gave her an almighty kick, right in the crotch.

Jane rolled around in agony. Eventually she managed to gasp: 'What the hell did you do that for?'

'Checking for bees!' said Tarzan.

Two sperm are in a body looking for an egg when one of them starts to wonder why it is taking so long. He asks the other sperm: 'Aren't we near the uterus yet?'

'No,' replied the other sperm, 'we haven't even got to the oesophagus.'

A man decided to have a facelift for his birthday. He spent $5000 and felt really good about the result. On his way home he stopped at a newsstand to buy a paper. Before leaving he said to the sales clerk: 'I hope you don't mind me asking, but how old do you think I am?'

'About 35,' was the reply.

'I'm actually 47,' the man said, feeling really happy.

After that he went into McDonald's for lunch and asked the order-taker the same question, to which the reply was: 'Oh, you look about 29.'

'I'm actually 47.' This made him feel really good.

While standing at the bus stop he asked an old woman the same question. She replied: 'I am 85 years old and my eyesight is going. But when I was young there was a sure way of telling a man's age. If I put my hand down your pants and play with your balls for ten minutes I will be able to tell your exact age.'

As there was no one around, the man thought, what the hell, and let her slip her hand down his pants. Ten minutes later the old lady said: 'Okay, I'm done. You are 47.'

Stunned, the man said: 'That's brilliant! How did you do that?'

The old lady replied: 'I was behind you in McDonald's.'

☆ ☆ ☆

A bloke was having a few drinks by himself at a casino when he met up with a striking but quite small and slim young woman. They got on famously and ended up in bed.

She told him she was a jockey and that, if he came to the races at Randwick that day, she'd tip him the winner of each race she was riding in by giving him a sign as she rode out of the saddling paddock.

In Race 2, she rode out rubbing both her tits. The bloke looked through the race book and found Two Abreast, on which he placed a hundred bucks at 5-1. It won by two lengths.

'Fuck, this is great!' he thought.

In Race 4, she rode out rubbing her fingers around her eyes. He put the lot on Eyeliner at 10-1 and was five grand in front.

In the last race she came out standing up in the stirrups and rubbing her pussy. He backed nothing.

After the races he met up with her and thanked her for the winners in races 2 and 4.

'What about Itchy Mickey in the last at 66-1?' she asked.

'Shit,' he said, 'I thought you were telling me the cunt was scratched.'

*　　*　　*

A koala visits Kings Cross and approaches a prostitute. She takes him up a dingy stairway into a small room and shows him a good time.

Afterwards the koala adjusts his fur and is about to leave. The prostitute says: 'Hey, mate, what about my money?'

As it's his first time in the city, the koala is puzzled. What can she mean? So the prostitute pulls a small dictionary out of her purse and points to the word 'prostitute'. Included in the definition is: 'Has sex and gets paid'. Whereupon the koala borrows the dictionary and turns to the word 'koala'.

She reads the definition: 'Eats bush, shoots and leaves'.

☆   ☆   ☆

While watching the TV, Dad is flicking peanuts in the air and catching them in his mouth. Distracted by a Kmart commercial for women's lingerie, he misjudges and gets a peanut stuck in his ear. It is very painful and his wife can't get it out. So he's heading for the front door to drive to St Vincent's when his daughter and her boyfriend arrive.

'Where are you going?' asks the daughter.

'To hospital. I've got a peanut stuck in my ear.'

'Let me take a look at that,' says the boyfriend. 'I reckon I could get it out.'

So the boyfriend grabs Dad by his head, sticks his fingers up his nose to pull his head back, and smacks him on the back of his head, knocking the peanut free.

'Well,' says Mum, 'our daughter has picked a good boy this time. No wonder he's studying to be a doctor.'

And the father replies: 'Yeah, and by the smell of his fingers he's going to be our son-in-law.'

They were on their honeymoon. Before consummating their marriage vows the husband threw his pants at her. 'Put these on,' he commanded.

'But they're much too big. I could never wear them.'

'That's right,' he said. 'I wear the pants in this family and don't you ever forget it.'

So she removed her tiny panties and tossed them to him. 'Put these on,' she said. He picked them up and slipped them over one foot but couldn't get them any higher than his knees. 'They're too tight. I'll never get into these.'

'That's right,' said his bride, 'and that's the way it's going to be until you change your bloody attitude.'

A woman went to see her psychiatrist. 'I'm really worried,' she said. 'Yesterday I found my daughter and the little boy next door together, naked, examining each other's bodies and giggling.'

The psychiatrist patted her hand and said: 'That's nothing to worry about. It's pretty normal.'

'Is it?' asked the woman. 'Well, it worries me. And it worries my son-in-law, too.'

☆   ☆   ☆

The new US ambassador was being briefed by an African politician on what his country had received from the Soviet Union before its collapse.

'The Russians built us a power plant, a highway and an airport. And we learnt how to drink vodka and play Russian roulette.'

The ambassador suggested that Russian roulette wasn't a very nice game.

'That's why we developed African roulette,' said the politician, with a hospitable smile. 'If you want to have good relations with our country, you'll have to play. Let me show you how.'

267

He clapped his hands and a moment later six astonishingly beautiful and entirely naked women were ushered in. 'You can choose any one of these women to give you oral sex,' he told the diplomat.

'That's great. But it doesn't seem very much like Russian roulette.'

'Oh, yes it is. You see, one of them is a cannibal.'

✷   ✷   ✷

The husband usually went out on a Friday night to play cards with his mates. But on this Friday he felt a bit crook and so was watching *Burke's Backyard* with his wife, who seemed strained and nervous. Right in the middle of the celebrity gardener section the phone rang. 'Don't answer it,' said the wife rather anxiously. But the husband picked up the receiver, listened for a few seconds and said: 'I've no fuckin' idea. Why don't you call the bloody coastguard?' And slammed the receiver down.

'Who was that?' asked his wife, her eyes wide with anxiety.

'I dunno,' said the husband. 'Some dickhead wanted to know if the coast was clear.'

Why is air a lot like sex?
Because it's no big deal unless you're not getting any.

A bloke suffering a bout of sexual dysfunction had considered every option. Viagra was unsuccessful so he investigated the possibility of a penile implant. But the thought of the paraphernalia was anti-libidinous. So he approached a Chinese herbalist who said that, yes, he could help. But it would require a different approach to sexual intercourse. He would, the herbalist said, have to learn to fuck like a Chinaman.

'And how do I do that?'

'It's very easy. Before you climb into bed with your wife you will read a few verses of Confucius.

This should enable you to begin the sexual act. But no sooner have you begun than you will withdraw and read this little pamphlet on Feng Shui. Then, you may resume where you left off. But before you get too aroused ...'

'You mean I'll be aroused?'

'Most certainly. But before you get *too* aroused, it is time to climb out of bed and write a verse of poetry on some spiritually elevating topic. Then you can resume.'

'And what happens then?'

'After a few seconds you withdraw, go to the kitchen and make some Chinese tea. Then you can return to the bed.'

'And then?'

'Then? It is time for some scroll painting. In the beginning it might be wise to paint something simple, like some stalks of bamboo. You'll find it's possible to paint bamboo leaves with single, deft brush-strokes. Now you return to the bed and ...'

'I return to the bed and ... ?'

'And having resumed, you stop again. And you consider the plight of the panda.'

'The plight of the panda?'

'Yes, the plight of the panda.'

There were other instructions and the man decided to follow them faithfully. So, that very evening, he read a few verses from Confucius. He then resumed congress, only to withdraw and study a pamphlet on Feng Shui.

No sooner was he back in the saddle than he dismounted to write a verse of poetry. And having returned to her arms, he almost immediately departed to brew some Chinese tea.

The coupling and uncoupling continued, to allow him opportunities to do some scroll painting and to consider the plight of the panda.

Finally, his wife had had enough. 'Christ!' she screamed. 'You know what's wrong with you, don't you. You fuck like a fucking Chinaman!'

The husband emerged from the bathroom naked and was climbing into bed when his wife complained, as usual: 'I have a headache.'

'Perfect,' her husband said. 'I was just in the bathroom powdering my dick with aspirin.'

*　*　*

A husband comes home to find his wife in the living room with her suitcases packed. 'Where the hell do you think you're going?' he asks.

'I'm going to Las Vegas. You can earn $400 for a blow job there, and I figured that I might as well earn money for what I do to you for free!'

The husband thinks for a moment, goes upstairs, and comes back down with his suitcase packed as well.

'Where do you think you're going?' the wife exclaims.

'I'm coming with you. I want to see how you survive on $800 a year!'

*　*　*

A very elderly couple is having an elegant dinner to celebrate their 70th wedding anniversary. The old man leans forward and says softly to his wife: 'Dear, there is something I must ask you. It has always bothered me that our tenth child never quite looked like the rest of our children. Now I want to assure you that these 70 years have been the most wonderful experience I could ever have hoped for, and your answer cannot take all that away. But I must know, did he have a different father?'

The wife drops her head, unable to look her husband in the eye. She pauses for a moment and then confesses: 'Yes. Yes, he did.'

The old man is very shaken. The reality of what his wife is admitting hits him harder than he had expected. With a tear in his eye he asks: 'Who ... who was he? Who was the father?'

Again the old woman drops her head, saying nothing at first as she tries to muster the courage to tell the truth to her husband. Then, finally, she says: 'You.'

Gretchen asks her husband if he'd like some

breakfast: grapefruit? Bacon, eggs, perhaps a slice of toast? Coffee to follow?

He declines. 'It's this Viagra,' he says. 'It's really taken the edge off my appetite.'

At lunchtime, she asks if he would like something. A bowl of homemade soup maybe, a cheese sandwich? Perhaps a plate of snacks and a glass of milk?

He declines. 'It's this Viagra,' he says. 'It's really taken the edge off my appetite.'

Come teatime, she asks if he wants anything to eat. She'll go to the cafe and buy him a burger. Maybe a steak pie. Or perhaps he'd like a pizza? How about a stir-fry? That would only take a couple of minutes.

He declines. 'It's this Viagra,' he says. 'It's really taken the edge off my appetite.'

'Well,' she says, 'would you mind getting off me? I'm starving!!'

☆ ☆ ☆

Back in the early 1960s, a young fellow walks into a talent agent's office and says he wants to break into showbiz. So the agent says: 'Okay, kid, show me what you can do.'

The kid tells some jokes, does a little soft shoe, sings a bit, does an acrobatic act with an ottoman, and is good enough to impress the agent. 'Great, kid! Just great!' says the agent. 'I can do things for ya! I think I can get you on a show on TV. By the way, what's your name?'

The young man, proud and excited, exclaims: 'Penis Van Lesbian.'

'Excuse me?' questions the agent.

'My name is Penis Van Lesbian.'

'Hey, I'm sorry kid, you're gonna have to change your name. Nobody is gonna hire you with a name like Penis Van Lesbian.'

Well, the young man is crestfallen, but steadfastly refuses to change his name, so he leaves to find another agent. A few months later he returns to the same agent.

'Hey kid! Good to see ya again!' says the agent. 'Are you still looking for work? Have you changed your name?'

With his head hanging low the young man

replies: 'Yes, every agent in town turned me down because of my name, Penis Van Lesbian. So I've changed it.'

'Great kid, great! What's your new name?'

'Dick Van Dyke!'

It's the year 2222 and Mike and Maureen land on Mars after accumulating enough frequent flyer points. They meet a Martian couple and are talking about all sorts of things. Mike asks if Mars has a stockmarket, if they have laptop computers, how they make money etc. Finally, Maureen brings up the subject of sex. 'Just how do you guys do it?' asks Maureen. The Martian responds: 'Pretty much the way you do.' A discussion ensues and finally the couples decide to swap partners for a night and experience one another.

Maureen and the male Martian go off to a bedroom, where the Martian strips. He's got only a teeny, weeny member – about 1 centimetre long and just 5 millimetres thick. 'I don't think this is going to work,' says Maureen.

'Why?' he asks. 'What's the matter?'

'Well,' she replies, 'it's just not long enough to reach me!'

'No problem,' he says, and proceeds to slap his forehead with his palm. With each slap of his forehead, his member grows until it's quite impressively long. 'Well,' she says, 'that's quite impressive, but it's still pretty narrow.'

'No problem,' he says, and starts pulling his ears. With each pull his member grows wider and wider until the entire measurement is extremely exciting to the woman.

'Wow!' she exclaims, as they fall into bed and make mad, passionate love.

The next day the couple rejoin their usual partners and go their separate ways. As they walk along Mike asks: 'Well, was it any good?'

'I hate to say it,' says Maureen, 'but it was pretty wonderful. How about you?'

'It was horrible,' he replied. 'All I got was a

headache ... she kept slapping my forehead and pulling my ears.'

Every time the married couple had sex the husband insisted on switching off the lights. The wife felt this was silly and thought she'd try to break him of the habit. So one night, while they were in the middle of making love, she turned on the light and looked down and saw her husband holding a dildo. She got very upset.

'You impotent bastard!' she screamed at him. 'How could you lie to me all these years. Explain yourself!'

The husband looked her in the eyes and said: 'Okay, I'll explain the dildo if you explain our three kids.'

A man who lived in a high-rise apartment building thought it was raining and put his hand out of the window to check. As he did so, a glass eye fell into his hand.

He looked up to see where it came from in time to see a girl looking down. 'Is this yours?' he asked.

She said: 'Yes, could you bring it up?' and the man agreed.

On his arrival, she was profuse in her thanks and offered him a drink. She was very attractive, and he agreed.

Shortly afterwards she said: 'I'm about to have dinner. There's plenty; would you like to join me?' He readily accepted her offer and both enjoyed a lovely meal.

As the evening was drawing to a close the girl said: 'I have had a marvellous evening. Would you like to stay the night?'

The man hesitated, then asked: 'Do you treat every man you meet like this?'

'No,' she replied, 'only those who catch my eye!'

A recalcitrant husband returned from a night at the pub. Knowing he'd be in big trouble with his wife, he decided to curry favour. So he tiptoed into the bedroom, burrowed under the blankets and began giving her oral sex. She made all sorts of happy little noises.

Afterwards he went into the bathroom to brush his teeth and, turning on the light, saw his wife sitting on the toilet.

'What are you doing here?' he asked in astonishment.

'Shhh,' she whispered, 'you'll wake Mother.'

I

INDOOR SPORTS

INFORMATION SYSTEMS

INDOOR SPORTS

A misguided golf ball drifts from a fairway over a high mesh fence, across a busy road and smashes through the front window of a suburban house. It knocks the owner unconscious and, ricocheting off his head, smashes an old vase.

When the owner awakes he finds a figure bending over him. 'Good afternoon, I'm a genie that has just been released from a vase after a thousand years of incarceration. To express my gratitude I would like to grant you a wish.'

'Bewdy!' says the bruised bloke. 'I'd like a million dollars.'

'Wish granted. The next time you check your bank statement you will find there's been a $1 million pay-in.'

At this point the wife enters the room. She sees the broken window, the broken vase, the bruised husband and the mysterious visitor. Her husband tells her about the million dollars and she points out that it was, after all, her vase.

'Then what boon do you crave?' says the genie. 'Your merest whim is my command!'

'I'd like a beautiful mansion in every capital city in the country. One in Perth, one in Adelaide, one in Brisbane, one in ...'

'Wish granted! I'll have my lawyers deliver the title deeds.'

The wife notices that the genie is staring at her. 'What is it?'

'Well, I've been locked up in that vase for a very long time. I haven't had sex in a thousand years.'

The woman looks at her husband.

'Well, I've got a million dollars. I don't really mind,' he says.

And she says: 'And I've got mansions in every capital city, so ... it's probably the least I can do.'

So the genie goes upstairs with the wife and, half an hour later, returns.

'How old are you, sir?' he inquires of the husband.

'Forty-eight.'

'Isn't that a little old to believe in genies?'

INFORMATION SYSTEMS

ISDN: It Still Does Nothing

APPLE: Arrogance Produces Profit-Losing Entity

DOS: Defective Operating System

BASIC: Bill's Attempt to Seize Industry Control

IBM: I Blame Microsoft

CD ROM: Consumer Device Rendered Obsolete in Months

WWW: World Wide Wait

MACINTOSH: Most Applications Crash: If Not, The Operating System Hangs

PENTIUM: Produces Erroneous Numbers Through Incorrect Understanding of Mathematics

WINDOWS: Will Install Needless Data On Whole System

MICROSOFT: Most Intelligent Customers Realise Our Software Only Fools Teenagers

* * *

State-of-the-Art: Any computer you can't afford.

Obsolete: Any computer you own.

Microsecond: The time it takes for your state-of-the-art computer to become obsolete.

Keyboard: The standard way to generate computer errors.

Mouse: An advanced input device to make computer errors easier to generate.

Floppy: The state of your wallet after purchasing a computer.

Portable Computer: A device invented to force

businessmen to work at home, on vacation and on business trips.

System Update: A quick method of trashing all your software.

A language instructor was explaining to her class that French nouns, unlike their English counterparts, are grammatically designated as masculine or feminine. Things like 'chalk' or 'pencil', she said, would have a gender association, although in English these words were neutral.

Puzzled, one student raised his hand and asked: 'What gender is a computer?'

The teacher wasn't certain which it was, and so divided the class into two groups and asked them to decide if a computer should be masculine or feminine. One group was comprised of the women in the class, and the other of the men. Both groups were asked to give four reasons for their recommendation.

The group of women concluded that computers should be referred to in the masculine gender because:

1 In order to get their attention, you have to turn them on.
2 They have a lot of data but are still clueless.
3 They are supposed to help you solve your problems, but half the time they *are* the problem.
4 As soon as you commit to one, you realise that, had you waited a little longer, you could have had a better model.

The men, on the other hand, decided that computers should definitely be referred to in the feminine gender because:

1 No one but their creator understands their internal logic.
2 The native language they use to communicate with other computers is incomprehensible to everyone else.
3 Even your smallest mistakes are stored in long-term memory for later retrieval.

4 As soon as you make a commitment to one you find yourself spending half your pay on accessories for it.

A KICK IN THE BALLS

A KICK
IN THE BALLS

A recent study conducted by Peter Reith's Department of Industrial Affairs has produced fascinating material on people's recreational preferences.

1 Increasingly, the sport of choice for the unemployed or incarcerated is: Basketball.
2 The sport of choice for maintenance level employees is: Football.
3 The sport of choice for front line workers is: Bowling.
4 The sport of choice for supervisors is: Baseball.
5 The sport of choice for middle management is: Tennis.
6 The sport of choice for corporate officers is: Golf.

The report concludes: The higher you are in the corporate structure, the smaller your balls.

* * *

A man with no arms or legs is lying on a beach when three beautiful women come up to him. The first one says: 'Have you ever been hugged?' He says no. And the woman hugs him.

The second one says: 'Have you ever been kissed?' He says no. And the woman kisses him.

And the third one says: 'Have you ever been fucked?' He says no. And she says: 'Well, you are now. The tide's coming in.'

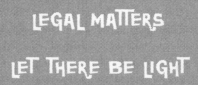

LEGAL MATTERS

LET THERE BE LIGHT

LEGAL MATTERS

Lawyer: 'Before you signed the death certificate, had you taken the pulse?'

Pathologist: 'No.'

Lawyer: 'Did you listen to the heart?'

Pathologist: 'No.'

Lawyer: 'Did you check for breathing?'

Pathologist: 'No.'

Lawyer: 'So, when you signed the death certificate you weren't sure he was dead, were you?'

Pathologist: 'Well, let me put it this way. The man's brain was in a jar on my desk. But I guess it's possible he could be out there practising law somewhere.'

After he has been on Death Row for years it is finally time to execute the murderer. All appeals have been exhausted. The governor has denied him clemency. And he's got the hiccups. He's got the hiccups as he walks between the cells of the condemned, a Dead Man Walking. He's got the hiccups when the priest gives him the Last Rites. He's still got the hiccups when they strap him into the electric chair. And just before the warder pulls the switch he says: 'Do you have any last requests?' And the guy says: 'Hic-yeah-hic. For chrissake, hic, do something to scare me.'

LET THERE BE LIGHT

How many Microsoft programmers does it take to change a light bulb?

None. Darkness becomes the standard.

* * *

How many dogs does it take to change a light bulb?

Golden retriever: The sun is shining, the day is young, we've got our whole lives ahead of us, and you're worrying about a bloody burnt-out light bulb?

Dachsund: I can't reach the light!

Toy poodle: I'll just blow in the border collie's ear and he'll do it. And by the time he's finished rewiring the house, my nails will be dry.

Rottweiler: Go ahead! Make me!

Border collie: Just one. And I'll replace any wiring that is in breach of standards.

Shi-tzu: Puh-leeze, dah-ling. Call the servants.

Labrador: Oh, me, me!!! Pleaseeeee. Let me change the light bulb? Can I? Can I!? Huh? Huh? Can I??

Cocker spaniel: Why bother? I can still pee on the carpet in the dark.

Mastiff: Mastiffs are not afraid of the dark.

Pointer: I see it. There it is, right there ...

Greyhound: It isn't moving, who cares?

Kelpie: Put all the light bulbs in a little circle ...

How many cockroaches does it take to change a light bulb?

I don't know. When you turn the light on, they all scatter.

How many men does it take to change a light bulb?

None. Let the bitch cook in the dark.

How many flies does it take to screw in a light bulb?
Just two. But I don't know how they got in there.

* * *

How many members of the USS *Enterprise* does it take to change a light bulb?
Eight. Scottie will report to Captain Kirk that the light bulb in the Engineering Section is burnt out, to which Kirk will send Bones to pronounce the light bulb dead. Scottie, after checking around, notices they have no more new light bulbs, and complains that he can't see in the dark to tend his engines. Kirk must make an emergency stop at the next uncharted planet, Alpha Regular IV, to procure a light bulb from the natives. Kirk, Spock, Bones, Sulu and three red-shirt security officers beam down. The three security officers are promptly killed by the natives and the rest of the landing party is captured. Meanwhile, back in orbit, Scottie notices a Klingon ship approaching and must warp out of orbit to escape detection. Bones cures the native king, who was

suffering from the flu, and as a reward the landing party is set free and given all the light bulbs they can carry. Scottie cripples the Klingon ship and walks back to the planet just in time to beam up Kirk *et al.* The new bulb is inserted and the *Enterprise* continues with its five-year mission.

✳   ✳   ✳

How many straight men from Oxford Street does it take to change a light bulb?
Both of them.

How many Melbourne Uni students does it take to change a light bulb?
Just one. He holds the light bulb and the universe revolves around him.

How many WASPs does it take to change a light bulb?
Two. One to call the electrician and one to mix the martinis.

How many people from New Jersey does it take to change a light bulb?
Three. One to change the bulb, one to witness and the third to shoot the witness.

M

MARITAL BLISS

MATTERS OF JUDGEMENT

MEDICAL MATTERS

MOTORING MATTERS

MULTICULTURALISM

MARITAL BLISS

A man inserted an advertisement in the classifieds. 'Wife wanted'. The next day he received 100 letters, all saying the same thing: 'You can have mine.'

*　*　*

A woman was drying herself after a shower when she suddenly slipped and landed spreadeagled on the bathroom floor. She tried to stand up but had landed so hard that her crotch had stuck to the tiles, creating a vacuum that prevented movement.

She called out to her husband, who tried with all his strength but she wouldn't budge. So he went next door and got his neighbour. They both pulled like oxen but couldn't lift her. She was absolutely stuck to the floor.

So the neighbour said: 'Why don't we just get

a hammer and break the floor tiles around her?'

'No, let's slide her into the kitchen,' said the husband. 'The tiles are cheaper in there.'

A woman bursts through the front door and says: 'Pack your bags, darling. I just won the lottery!'

And the husband says: 'Great! Should I pack for the beach or the mountains?'

She says: 'I don't give a stuff. Just go to buggery!'

Son: 'Is it true, Dad, that in some parts of Africa a man doesn't know his wife until he marries her?'
Dad: 'That happens in every country, son.'

I never knew what real happiness was until I got married; then it was too late.

Marriage is the triumph of imagination over intelligence.
Second marriage is the triumph of hope over experience.

If you want your spouse to listen and pay strict attention to every word you say, talk in your sleep.

It's not true that married men live longer than single men. It only seems longer.

If it weren't for marriage, men would go through life thinking they had no faults at all.

Why is divorce so expensive?
Because it's worth it.

An elderly couple were preparing for bed one night when the husband said: 'Darling, you should go bra-less.'

The wife was delighted. 'So you think my breasts are still good enough to go bra-less?'

He replied: 'No, but maybe it'll pull the wrinkles out of your face.'

A married couple were involved in a serious car accident. Before he could drag his wife from the vehicle, the car caught fire and the woman's face was burned. Later the doctor told the husband they couldn't graft any skin from her body because she was too thin. So he offered to donate some of his own. But the only skin on his body the doctor felt was suitable would have to come from his buttocks. The husband promised his wife that he'd tell no one where the skin came from and the doctor and his nursing staff promised to keep their secret.

After the surgery was completed, everyone was astonished by the woman's radiance. She'd never looked so beautiful before. All her friends and relatives went on and on about her wonderful complexion.

One evening, alone with her husband, she was thanking him profusely for his sacrifice. 'Darling, there is no way I could ever repay you.'

'Don't worry, darling,' he said. 'I get all the thanks I need every time I see your mother kiss you on the cheek.'

* * *

A wife wakes in the middle of the night to find her husband missing from bed. She checks around the house and finds him in the basement sobbing.

'Honey, what's wrong?' she asks.

He says: 'Remember, twenty years ago, I got you pregnant? And your father threatened me to marry you or to go to jail?'

'Yes, of course, darling.'

'Well, I would have been released tonight.'

MATTERS OF JUDGEMENT

It was a big Irish wedding, where, according to tradition, everyone got pissed and the bride and groom's families had a row and began wrecking the reception room and generally kicking the crap out of each other. The police got called in to break up the fight and, the next week, all the wedding guests appeared in court. The fight flared up in the courtroom again until the judge brought calm with enthusiastic use of his hammer and much shouting of 'Silence in court!'

Whereupon Paddy, the best man, stood up and said: 'Your Honour, I was the best man at the wedding, and think I should explain what happened.'

The judge agreed and Paddy was sworn in.

'Your Majesty, it's a tradition at weddings in our district that the best man gets the first dance with the bride.'

The judge nodded and gestured for Paddy to continue.

'Well, Your Highness, after I'd finished the first dance the music kept going, so I kept dancing to the second song. And after that, the music kept going and I danced to the third song. When all of a sudden the groom leapt over the table, ran towards us and gave the bride an unmerciful kick in her private parts.'

The judge sat up and said: 'God, that must have hurt!'

And Paddy said: 'Hurt! He broke three of my fucking fingers!'

☆   ☆   ☆

A family court judge was interviewing a woman about her proposed divorce. He asked: 'What are the grounds?'

She replied: 'About four acres with a nice little house in the middle. Oh, yes, and a little stream running by.'

'No,' he said, 'I meant what was the foundation of this case.'

'Concrete. And the house itself is brick veneer.'

The judge was becoming exasperated. 'That's not what I mean! What are your relations like?'

'I've an aunt and uncle living in the suburb, and so do my husband's parents.'

The judge said: 'But do you have a real grudge?'

'No,' she replied, 'we just have a two-car carport. But it's fine for the Saab and the Volvo.'

'Please,' he tried again. 'Is there any infidelity in your marriage?'

'Yes, both my son and daughter have stereo sets. We don't necessarily like the music, but when they're playing rock'n'roll they'll sometimes wear headsets.'

'Madam, does your husband ever beat you up?'

'Yes. About twice a week he gets up much earlier than I do.'

Exploding in rage, the judge said: 'But why do you want a bloody divorce?'

'Oh, I don't want a divorce,' she said. 'I've never wanted a divorce. My husband does. He says he can't communicate with me.'

MEDICAL MATTERS

A woman was very distraught at the fact that she had not had a date or any sex for quite some time. Feeling something was wrong with her, she decided to employ the medical expertise of a sex therapist. Her GP recommended that she go and see Dr Chang, a well-known Chinese sex therapist. So she went to see him. Upon entering the examination room, Dr Chang said: 'Okay, take off all your crose. Now get down and crawl reery fass to the other side of the woom.' So she did.

Dr Chang said: 'Okay, now crawl reery fass to me.' So she did that too.

Dr Chang slowly shook his head and said: 'Your probrem vewy vewy bad. You haf Zachary Disease. Worse case I ever see, that why you not haf sex or dates.'

Confused, the woman asked: 'What is Zachary Disease?'

Dr Chang replied: 'It when your face rook Zachary rike your arse.'

✹　✹　✹

What's the difference between a doctor and God? God doesn't think he's a doctor.

✹　✹　✹

Doctor, doctor,' the woman said too loudly as she rushed into the room. 'I want you to say frankly what's wrong with me!'

Looking at her from head to foot he said: 'Madam, I've just three things to tell you.

'First, you must reduce your weight by 20 kilos.

'Secondly, you should use about a tenth as much make-up.

'And thirdly, I'm a portrait painter. The doctor lives upstairs.'

'Doctor, doctor, I need some pills. I've become a kleptomaniac.'
'Try these. And if they don't work, get me a CD player.'

'Doctor, doctor, every time I sit down I have hallucinations. I see visions of Mickey Mouse and Pluto. And every time I stand up, I see Donald Duck.'
'How long have you been having these Disney spells?'

A sceptical anthropologist was cataloguing South American folk remedies with the assistance of a tribal *brujo*, who indicated that the leaves of a particular fern were a sure cure for any case of constipation. When the anthropologist expressed his doubts, the *brujo* looked him in the eye and said: 'Let me tell you, with fronds like these, who needs enemas?'

An Indian chief was feeling very sick, so he summoned the medicine man. After a brief examination, the medicine man took out a long, thin strip of elk hide and gave it to the chief, instructing him to bite off, chew and swallow one inch of the leather every day. After a month, the medicine man returned to see how the chief was feeling. The chief shrugged and said: 'The thong is ended, but the malady lingers on.'

Pete complained to his friend: 'My elbow really hurts. I guess I should see a doctor.'

His friend said: 'Don't do that. There's a computer at the chemist's that can diagnose anything quicker and cheaper than a doctor. Simply put in a sample of your urine and the computer will diagnose your problem and tell you what you can do with it. And it only costs $10.'

So Pete filled a jar with urine and went to the chemist. He poured in the sample and deposited the $10. The computer started making noises, and the various lights started flashing. And out popped a small slip of paper which read: 'You have tennis elbow. Soak your arm in warm water. Avoid heavy labour. It will be better in two weeks.'

Thinking how amazing this new technology was and how it would change medical practice forever, he began to wonder if the computer could be fooled. So he mixed together some tap water, a stool sample from his dog and urine samples from his wife and daughter. To top it off, he masturbated into the concoction. He then went back to the chemist's, poured in the sample and deposited the $10. The machine printed out the following analysis:

'Your tap water is too hard. Get a water softener.

Your dog has ringworm. Bathe him in antifungal shampoo.

Your wife is pregnant with twin girls. They aren't yours. Get a lawyer.

Your daughter is using cocaine. Put her in a rehabilitation clinic.

And if you don't stop jerking off, your tennis elbow will never get better.'

✸ ✸ ✸

Fred goes to a doctor and says: 'Doctor, I want to be castrated.'

The doctor says: 'Look, I don't know what kind of cult you're into or what your motives are, but I'm not going to do that sort of operation.'

Fred says: 'Doctor, I just want to be castrated, and I'm a little embarrassed talking about it, but I have $5000 cash right here. Will you do it?'

The doctor says: 'Well, okay. I guess I could make this one exception. I don't understand it, but okay.'

So he puts Fred to sleep, does the operation and is waiting at the bedside when Fred wakes up. 'Well, Doc, how did it go?' Fred asks.

'It went fine, just fine. It's really not too difficult an operation. As a matter of fact, $5000 is a lot to pay for such a simple task and I felt a little guilty taking that much. So while I was operating I also noticed that you had never been circumcised, so I went ahead and did that too. I think it's really better for a man to be circumcised, and I hope you don't mind ...'

'CIRCUMCISED!' yells Fred. 'THAT'S the word!'

* * *

I've been feeling very, very depressed lately. In fact, when I woke up this morning I felt so bad that I decided to kill myself by taking 60 Aspros.'

'What happened?'

'Well, after the first two I felt much better.'

* * *

Howard had felt guilty all day long. No matter how much he tried to forget about it, he couldn't. The guilt and sense of betrayal were overwhelming.

But every once in a while he'd hear that soothing

voice trying to reassure him: 'Howard. Don't worry about it. You aren't the first doctor to sleep with one of his patients and you won't be the last ...'

But invariably the other voice would bring him back to reality. 'Howard, you're a veterinarian.'

*   *   *

A beautiful, voluptuous woman goes to a gynaecologist. The doctor takes one look at the woman and all his professionalism goes out the window. Right away he tells her to undress. After she has disrobed he begins to stroke her thigh. As he does this he says to the woman: 'Do you know what I'm doing?'

'Yes,' she says, 'you're checking for any abrasions or dermatological abnormalities.'

'That's right,' says the doctor. He then begins to fondle her breasts. 'Do you know what I'm doing now?' he says.

'Yes,' says the woman, 'you're checking for any lumps or breast cancer.'

'Correct,' replies the doctor. He then begins to

have sexual intercourse with the woman. He says to her: 'Do you know what I'm doing now?'

'Yes,' she says, 'you're getting herpes.'

✲   ✲   ✲

Hello, welcome to the Psychiatric Hotline.

If you are obsessive-compulsive, please press 1 repeatedly.

If you are co-dependent, please ask someone to press 2.

If you have multiple personalities, please press 3, 4, 5 and 6.

If you are paranoid-delusional, we know who you are and what you want. Just stay on the line so we can trace the call.

If you are schizophrenic, listen carefully and a little voice will tell you which number to press.

If you are manic-depressive, it doesn't matter which number you press. No one will answer.

If you are anxious, just start pressing numbers at random.

If you are phobic, don't press anything.

If you are anal-retentive, please hold.

A son takes his father to the doctor. The doctor gives them the bad news that the father is dying of cancer. The father tells the son that he has had a good long life and wants to stop at the pub on the way home to celebrate it.

While at the pub, the father sees several of his friends. He tells them that he is dying of AIDS.

When the friends leave, the son says: 'Dad, you are dying of cancer. Why did you tell them that you're dying of AIDS?'

The father replies: 'I don't want them fucking your mother after I'm gone!'

A man walks into a pharmacy and asks the woman behind the counter: 'Is there a male pharmacist available?'

'No,' she says, 'my sister and I own this place and we are both pharmacists. How can we help you?'

The man steps back and opens his coat, revealing a rather large bulge in the front of his pants and says: 'It's been like this for seven days now. Can you give me anything for it?'

'Hmmm,' says the woman, 'let me go and consult my sister.'

Moments later she returns and says: 'Okay, we'll give you $400 cash and a half-interest in the pharmacy.'

★　★　★

A man is urinating one day when the end of his penis drops off.

He thinks: 'This is probably not a good thing.' So he picks up the knobby end and sticks it in his pocket, then races off to the doctor. He waits in the surgery for a while, then he's called in.

The doctor greets him and asks: 'What's the problem?'

'Well, doctor, I was urinating and the knob fell off. Here it is.' And he reaches into his pocket and hands the piece to the doctor.

The doctor looks, frowns, and then replies: 'What are you talking about? This is a marshmallow!'

'Well, that can't be right! I ate my last marsh-mallow on the way here!'

A man visits his doctor. 'I think I have a problem, doc,' says the man. 'One of my balls has turned blue.'

The doctor examines him briefly and concludes the patient will die if he doesn't have his testicle removed.

'Are you crazy?' exclaims the man. 'How could I let you do such a thing to me?'

'Do you want to die?' asks the doctor rhetorically, and the patient has to agree to have his testicle removed. But two weeks after the operation he comes back.

'Doc, I don't know how to say this, but the other ball has turned blue too.'

The doctor tells him that if he wants to live, his other testicle must be cut off too. And again, the man is very reluctant. 'Hey, do you want to die?' asks the doctor, and the patient agrees to have the operation.

But, about two weeks after he is testicle-less, he returns to the doctor. 'I think something is very wrong with me. My penis is now completely blue.'

After briefly examining the patient once again, the doctor gives him the bad news. If he wants to live, his penis has to go.

Of course, he doesn't want to hear about it. 'You really want to die?' asks the doctor.

'But ... how do I pee?'

'We'll install a plastic pipe, and there'll be no problem.'

So, the penis is removed and a while after the operation the unfortunate man again returns to the doctor's office. He is very angry.

'Doctor, the plastic pipe turned blue.'

'What?'

'Can you tell me what the hell's happening?'

So the doctor examines the patient more carefully this time and says: 'Hmmm, I think it's the dye from your jeans ...'

* * *

Harry answers the telephone. It's an ER doctor.

The doctor says: 'Your wife was in a serious car accident and I have bad news and good news. The bad news is she has lost all use of both arms and legs and will need help eating and going to the toilet for the rest of her life.'

Harry says: 'My God. What's the good news?'

The doctor says: 'I'm kidding. She's dead!'

* * *

A bloke had a major argument with his girlfriend. He was in the wrong, but not enough to back down.

So, after storming away, and cooling off, the bloke had a think. He was clearly in the wrong and felt pretty guilty about all the trauma it had caused.

So to make it up to his girlfriend, he said he'd buy her a gift.

'Anything at all, my love,' the bloke said, overcome with remorse.

'Oh, I don't know,' she replied. 'You really needn't do this. But, if you must, just get me something really expensive I don't need.'

The following day he booked her in for chemotherapy.

MOTORING MATTERS

A man was speeding down the highway, feeling secure in a group of cars all travelling at the same speed. However, as they passed a speed trap, he got caught with an infrared speed detector and was pulled over. The officer handed him a notice, received his signature and was about to walk away when the man asked: 'Officer, I know I was speeding but I don't think it's fair – there were plenty of other cars around me that were going just as fast, so why did I get the ticket?'

'Ever go fishing?' the policeman suddenly asked the man.

'Um, yeah ...' the startled man replied.

The officer grinned and added: 'Did you ever catch all the fish?'

MULTICULTURALISM

A bus stops and two Italian men get on. They seat themselves and engage in animated conversation. The lady sitting behind them ignores them at first, but her attention is galvanised when she hears one of the men say: 'Emma come first. Denna I come. Two asses, they come together. I come again. Two asses, they come together again. I come again and pee twice. Then I come once-a-more.'

'You foul-mouthed swine,' retorts the lady very indignantly. 'In this country we don't talk about our sex lives in public.'

'Hey, coola down lady,' says the man. 'Imma just tellun my friend howa to spell Mississippi.'

A Chinese guy does his shopping at a Greek greengrocer's. The Greek keeps picking on the Chinese because he can't pronounce the letter 'r'.

'It's Friday, you stupid prick, not Fliday.'

'Yeah yeah yeah, Fliday.'

After three months the Chinese has had enough and starts practising how to say Friday. So the next time he goes to the greengrocer he says to the Greek: 'It's Friday, you Gleek plick.'

There's a big Italian funeral in Carlton. It takes about half an hour to wend its way up Lygon Street. A couple of mafiosi are standing on the footpath. One says: 'Whose funeral is that?'

'One of Big Louie's girlfriends.'

'What did she die of?'

'Gonorrhoea.'

'I didn't know you could die from gonorrhoea.'

'You can when you give it to Big Louie.'

A Pom, an Irishman and a Scot go out to a pub and order three pints. They each find a fly floating on the top of their mug.

The Pom says, 'Barman, can I have a spoon?' and quietly removes the fly from his brew.

The Irishman says, 'Get out of there!' and flicks the fly away with a finger.

The Scot picks up the fly with his fingers and says, 'All right ya wee fucker. Spit it out! Now!'

Two Irishmen were having a race to the top of a hill.

'If I get to the top of the hill first,' said one, 'I'm going to write my name on that tree.'

And the other said: 'If I get to the top first I'm going to rub it out.'

* * *

Two Irishmen were walking through the streets of Calcutta when they saw an old nun approaching. 'I wonder if that's Mother Teresa?'

'Let's ask her.'

So they asked her if she was the holy woman, to which she replied: 'Piss off, you Irish perverts.'

As they watched her walk away one Irishman turned to the other and said: 'Now we'll never know!'

Mary was a devout Catholic who, during the course of her marriage, had had 17 children. Then her husband died. Mary remarried a few months later and had another 22 children with her second husband. Finally, exhausted by childbirth and child-rearing, she died.

At the wake, the priest made a little speech about Mary and said: 'At last they're finally together.'

One of the mourners said: 'Excuse me, Father, but do you mean Mary and her first husband? Or Mary and her second husband?'

The priest said: 'I mean her legs!'

*   *   *

An Irishman had noticed that there was a lot of money in nostalgia. So he bought a million 1942 calendars for 20 quid. 'What on earth are you going to do with them?' he was asked.

'When 1942 comes back, I'll make a fortune.'

*   *   *

An Irishman is looking for a job with the forestry commission. The ranger takes the Irishman out to test his knowledge about trees. 'What's this one?'

'That's a she-oak.'

'What's this one?'

'That's a red gum.'

'Okay, you're going pretty well. But where's the front of that tree?'

'I beg your pardon?'

'Where is the front of that tree?'

The Irishman gets out of the ranger's 4WD, walks round the tree and climbs back in. 'It's the other side.'

'And how did you work that out?'
'Somebody's had a shit there.'

* * *

An Englishman, an Irishman and a Scotsman were sitting in a pub drinking and discussing how stupid their wives were.

Englishman: 'I tell you, my wife is so stupid. Last week she went to the supermarket and bought £300 worth of meat because it was on sale, and we don't even have a fridge to keep it in.'

Scotsman: 'Ma wife is thicker than that. Just last week she went oot and spent £17 000 on a new car, and she doesna even know how to drive.'

The Irishman nodded sagely and agreed that these two women sounded like they were both pretty stupid. However, he still thought his wife was dumber, and chuckles: 'Ah, it kills me every toime Oi tink of it. Moi woife just left to go on a holiday in Greece and Oi watched her packing her bag, and she must have put 100 condoms in there – and she doesn't even have a penis!'

*   *   *

Two Irishmen drove to a petrol station in Mildura for a fill-up. They'd heard rumours about a contest for people who purchased a full tank. So when they went inside to pay, they asked about it. 'If you win, you're entitled to free sex,' said the attendant.

'How do we enter?' asked the Irishmen.

'Well, I think of a number between one and ten. If you guess right, you win free sex.'

'Fine, fine,' said one Irishman. 'I guess seven.'

'Sorry, I was thinking of eight.'

Next week the two Irishmen returned to the same station. This time the other Irishman asked the attendant about the contest.

'I'm thinking of a number between one and ten,' he said. 'If you guess right, you win free sex.'

'Two,' said the Irishman.

'Sorry, I was thinking of three,' replied the attendant, 'but come back next week and try again.'

As they walked back to the car the first Irishman said to the other: 'I reckon this contest is rigged.'

'No it isn't,' said his friend. 'My wife won twice last week.'

*　*　*

Two Irish blokes, Paddy and Murphy, are in a bar in the wild west, totally skint. The barman shakes his head and says: 'I fucking hate Indians. Last week the bastards burnt my barn to the ground, raped my wife and killed my children.' He then says: 'If any man brings me the head of a Red Indian I'll give him $1000.'

The two Irish blokes look at each other and walk out of the bar to go searching for an Indian. They've been walking around for a while when suddenly they see one, so Paddy throws a stone which hits the Indian right on the head. The Indian falls off his horse but lands 20 metres down a ravine. So the two Irishmen make their way down the ravine where Paddy starts sawing the Indian's head off.

In the middle of doing this, Murphy says: 'Paddy, look.' To which Paddy replies: 'Not now, I'm busy.'

Murphy taps him on the shoulder and says: 'I really think you should look at this.'

Paddy keeps on sawing and says: 'Look, fuck off. You can see I'm busy – there's $1000 in my hand.'

But Murphy's adamant. 'Please, Paddy, look at this.' So Paddy looks up, and standing at the top of the ravine are 5000 Red Indians. Paddy shakes his head in disbelief and says: 'Fuck me! We're going to be millionaires!'

O'Reilly arrives at Tullamarine and wanders around the terminal with tears streaming down his cheeks. An Ansett employee asks him what's wrong.

'I've lost all me luggage.'

'All of it?'

'The lot.'

'Oh dear. How did that happen?'

'The cork fell out.'

An American soldier, serving in World War II, had just returned from several weeks of action on the German front lines. Finally granted R&R, he was on a train bound for London. The train was very crowded, so the soldier walked the length of the train, looking for an empty seat. The only unoccupied seat was directly adjacent to a well-dressed middle-aged lady and was being used by her little dog.

The war-weary soldier asked: 'Please, ma'am, may I sit in that seat?'

The Englishwoman looked down her nose at the soldier, sniffed and said: 'You Americans. You are such a rude class of people. Can't you see my little Fifi is using that seat?'

The soldier walked away, determined to find a place to rest, but after another trip down to the end of the train, found himself again facing the woman with the dog. Again he asked: 'Please, lady. May I sit there? I'm very tired.'

The Englishwoman wrinkled her nose and snorted: 'You Americans! Not only are you rude, you are also arrogant. Imagine!'

The soldier didn't say anything else; he leaned over, picked up the little dog, tossed it out the window of the train and sat down in the empty seat.

The woman shrieked and wailed, and demanded that someone defend her and chastise the soldier. An English gentleman sitting across the aisle spoke up. 'You know, sir, you Americans do seem to have a penchant for doing the wrong thing. You eat holding the fork in the wrong hand. You drive your autos on the wrong side of the road. And now, sir, you've thrown the wrong bitch out the window!'

Two African-Americans are walking down the street. One of them spots a sign reading 'TURN WHITE FOR 99 CENTS'. One has $1 and the other 98 cents. So the one with the dollar says: 'Look, I'll go in and try it. And when I come out, I'll give you my change.'

It's agreed, and the first man goes inside.

After a few minutes he comes out and, to his

friend's amazement, is totally white. 'Wow man! You are as white as any honky! Can I have that cent now?'

And he says: 'Go get a job, nigger.'

An Aborigine is walking through the park with a piece of corrugated iron under one arm and a billy under the other. A friend sees him and asks: 'How did you finish up with your divorce?'

And he replies: 'Pretty good. I got both home and contents.'

A white professor is sent to darkest Africa to live with a primitive tribe. He spends years with them, teaching them reading, writing, maths and science. One day the wife of the tribe's chief gives birth to a white child. The members of the tribe are shocked, and the chief pulls the professor aside and says: 'Look here! You're the only white man we've ever seen and this woman gave birth to a white child. It doesn't take a genius to figure out what happened!'

The professor replies: 'No, Chief. You're mistaken. What you have here is a natural occurrence... what we in the civilised world call an albino! Look at that field over there. All of the sheep are white except for one black one. Nature does this on occasion.'

The chief is silent for a moment, then says: 'Tell you what. You don't say anything more about the sheep and I won't say anything more about the baby.'

*　　*　　*

The following people become stranded on beautiful deserted islands in the middle of nowhere:

2 Italian men and 1 Italian woman
2 Frenchmen and 1 Frenchwoman
2 German men and 1 German woman
2 Greek men and 1 Greek woman
2 Englishmen and 1 Englishwoman

2 Bulgarian men and 1 Bulgarian woman

2 American men and 1 American woman

2 Japanese men and 1 Japanese woman

2 Irishmen and 1 Irishwoman

One month later, on these absolutely stunning deserted islands in the middle of nowhere, the following things have occurred:

One Italian man has killed the other Italian man for the Italian woman.

The two Frenchmen and the Frenchwoman are living happily together in a menage à trois.

The two German men have a strict weekly schedule of when they alternate with the German woman.

The two Greek men are sleeping with each other and the Greek woman is cleaning and cooking for them.

The two Englishmen are waiting for someone to introduce them to the Englishwoman.

The two Bulgarian men have taken a long look at

the endless ocean and one look at the Bulgarian woman and have started swimming.

The two American men are contemplating the virtues of suicide while the American woman keeps on bitching about her body being her own, the true nature of feminism, how she can do everything they can do, the necessity of fulfilment, the equal division of household chores, how her last boyfriend respected her opinion and treated her much nicer and how her relationship with her mother is improving. But at least the taxes are low and it isn't raining.

The two Japanese men have faxed Tokyo and are waiting for instructions.

The two Irishmen began by dividing the island into north and south and setting up a distillery. They do not remember if sex is in the picture because it gets sort of foggy after the first few litres of coconut whisky, but they are satisfied that at least the English are not getting any.

Why do Jewish men like to watch porno films backwards?
So they can see the hooker give back the money.

*   *   *

An old Jewish man from Vaucluse wins first prize in Lotto – $6 million. There's no sharing of the prize-money – it's all his. At the press conference, he explains that he doesn't need the money as he lives alone. Of his entire family, only he survived the Holocaust.

But Australia has been good to him, so he announces his intention of donating all the prize-money. 'I'll give $1 million to the Princess Diana fund for landmine victims. I'll give $1 million to the Royal Flying Doctor Service. I will give $1 million towards the maintenance of the Great Synagogue. I'll give $1 million to Rev. Noffs' Wayside Chapel. I will give $1 million to Amnesty International. And I will give $1 million to the Nazi Party.'

There was consternation at the press conference.

'But why the Nazi Party?' reporters chorused. 'Why them, of all people?'

The old bloke replies that it's the least he can do. He pulls up his sleeve and points to a tattoo. 'After all, they gave me the numbers.'

In deep financial trouble, Cohen went into the desert and called upon Jehovah. 'God, in all your glory what does a million dollars mean to you?'

Suddenly the clear blue sky was full of black clouds and Cohen heard a great voice booming from above. 'A penny.'

Then Cohen asked: 'And in terms of your omnipotence, what does a million years mean to you?'

To which God replied: 'A second.'

'Well then,' said Cohen, 'can I borrow a penny?'

To which God replied: 'In a second.'

Goldstein had started with just one gourmet food shop in Double Bay, but within a year, had dozens all over Sydney. Then he began franchising the concept until there were Goldstein Gourmet Shops all over Australia.

A customer marvelled at his brilliance. 'What makes you so smart?' she asked.

'Herring heads,' said Goldstein. 'Eat enough herring heads and you'll be brilliant.'

'Can I buy some here?'

'Certainly,' said Goldstein. 'They're $10 each.'

The lady took three. A week later she complained that her IQ was unchanged.

'You didn't eat enough yet,' said Goldstein.

So this time she took 20.

On her next visit, she complained bitterly that she was no more intelligent – and certainly no richer. 'In fact, this is costing me a fortune. You sell me a whole herring for $1 – why should I pay you so much for just the head?'

'You see,' said Goldstein. 'You're getting smarter already.'

* * *

A cashier from Westpac rang Mr Cohen. 'We called you up to tell you that as of the first day of this month your account appears to be overdrawn by $500.'

'So?'

'Mr Cohen, you're overdrawn $500!'

'Then please, you should look at your books and tell me how the account stood on the first day of last month.'

She checked the computer records. 'Well, on the first day of last month you had a balance to your credit of $32.50.'

'So?' shouted Cohen. 'And did I call you up?'

* * *

An African-American family was awaiting the return of the mother from her job cleaning the home of a film star in Beverly Hills. The little baby, yet to speak her first word, was becoming increasingly agitated.

Finally, the mother appeared in the doorway and the baby cried: 'Mother!'

Her father was immensely proud. 'Well, if that don't beat all! This kid is just so *smart*. She knows half a word already!'

A young man calls home and tells his Jewish mother that he has decided to go back into the closet because he has met a wonderful girl and they are going to be married. He tells his mother that he is sure she will be happier, since he knows that his gay lifestyle has been very disturbing to her.

She responds that she is indeed delighted and asks tentatively: 'I suppose it would be too much to hope that she is Jewish?'

He tells her that not only is the girl Jewish and comes from a wealthy family, but her father is a doctor.

She admits she is overwhelmed by the news, and asks: 'What's her name?'

He answers: 'Monica Lewinsky.'

There is a pause, then his mother asks: 'What happened to that nice black boy you were dating last year?'

*   *   *

Passionate kiss, like spider's web, soon lead to undoing of fly.

Virginity like bubble: one prick all gone.

Man who run in front of car get tired.

Man who run behind car get exhausted.

Man with hand in pocket feel cocky all day.

Foolish man give wife grand piano; wise man give wife upright organ.

Man who walk through airport turnstile sideways going to Bangkok.

Man with one chopstick go hungry.

Man who scratches arse should not bite fingernail.

Man who eat too many prunes get good run for money.

Baseball is wrong: man with four balls cannot walk.

Panties not best thing on earth but next to best thing on earth.

War doesn't determine who is right; war determines who is left.

Wife who put husband in doghouse soon find him in cathouse.

Man who fight with wife all day get no piece at night.

It takes many nails to build crib but one screw to fill it.

Man who drive like hell bound to get there.

Man who stand on toilet seat is high on pot.

Man who lives in glass house should change clothes in basement.

BIG NAMES

BIG NAMES

What's the difference between Christopher Reeve and O.J. Simpson?
Christopher Reeve got the electric chair. O.J. walked.

What's white and sticky and found on the bathroom wall?
George Michael's latest release.

How does Michael Jackson know it's time for bed?
When the big hand is on the little hand.

What's the difference between Michael Jackson and a plastic bag?
One is white, plastic and dangerous to young children. The other is a plastic bag.

How can you tell if Michael Jackson has company?

There's a big wheel parked outside his house.

How does Michael Jackson pick his nose?
From a catalogue.

How did Helen Keller's mother punish her?
By rearranging the furniture.

What's the difference between Princess Di and Tiger Woods?
He's got a better driver.

What did St Peter say to Di at the Pearly Gates?
'Wipe that Merc off your face.'

Why is Di like a mobile phone?
They both die in tunnels.

What is 14 metres long and has eight teeth?
The front row at a John Farnham concert.

What do you call four dogs with no balls?
The Spice Girls.

Heard of the new plans for a film about JFK Jr? It's called *Three Funerals and a Wedding*.

What did the Queen say when she heard Princess Diana died in a car smash?
'Was Fergie with her?'

Why did Elton John sing at Princess Di's funeral? Because he was the only queen who cared.

Elton John is to make a tribute record for Mother Teresa ...
'Sandals in the Bin'.

What did the French mortuary attendant say when he got the body bags?
'Zip-a-de Dodi, Zip-a-de Di.'

☆　　☆　　☆

Three midgets decide to submit their vital statistics to the *Guinness Book of Records*. The first says: 'I have very short arms.' And learns, a few weeks later, that he's been accepted.

The second one says: 'I've got very short legs.' And in due course, he's accepted as well.

The third one says: 'Well, I've got a very, very small penis.' Unfortunately he gets a knockback from the Guinness people. Bitterly disappointed, he asks the other midgets: 'Who the hell is Leonardo DiCaprio?'

☆   ☆   ☆

Bill Gates meets Hugh Grant at a Hollywood party. They get talking and Bill says: 'I've seen some great pictures of Divine Brown lately – I sure would like to get together with her!'

Hugh: 'Well, Bill. Ever since the publicity she got from the "meeting" I had with her, her price has gone through the roof.'

Bill (with a smug chuckle): 'Well Hugh, you know money really isn't a problem to me. What's her number?'

So Bill gets the number and sets up a date. Bill and Divine meet up and after they finish, Bill, lying there in a blissful state having a fag, whispers: 'God, that was great! Now I know why they call you Divine.'

To which Divine replies: 'Why thank you, Bill – and I finally got to know why you chose the name Microsoft!!'

☆   ☆   ☆

The McCartney kids are at the family ranch anxiously awaiting news of their mother. Paul emerges from his wife's bedroom. 'Kids, there's good news and bad news.

'The bad news is your mother's strength and will to live have been sucked away by her awful disease and she died a few moments ago.

'The good news is … it's steak and chips for dinner!'

☆   ☆   ☆

Jeff Kennett wakes up one morning feeling great. He walks into the bathroom and catches his reflection in the mirror. 'Lookin' good, Jeff!' he says to himself.

Then he steps into the shower and lifts his arm. 'Phweew! Something stinks,' he thinks to himself, so he scrubs himself down.

After his shower he still reeks, so he douses himself in deodorant and aftershave and heads down to breakfast.

Felicity looks up: 'Wow, Jeff, you're looking good this morning.'

'Yeah, I feel great. There's just this one problem ...'

'What's that?' she asks, approaching him.

'Phweew!' she recoils. 'Jeff, you've got to do something about that smell!'

'I don't know what to do! I'm wearing enough Old Spice to sink a ship!'

So he leaves home and heads into the office, hoping it won't be so noticeable, and he bumps into Alan Stockdale in the carpark.

'Jeffy-boy, lookin' good!'

'Yeah, and I feel great too. Just got this one problem ...'

'What's that?' he asks, approaching. 'Phweew! Jeff, you've gotta do something about that stench, we've got an important meeting soon! Go shower or something!'

'That's the problem, Alan, I've showered twice. I'm wearing about as much deodorant as I can and I still stink!'

'Well, go and see your doctor.'

So he does. The doctor pulls out his textbook. 'Let's see. Looks bad, feels bad, smells bad. Nope. Looks good, feels bad, smells bad. Nope, not that one. Ah, here we are ... Looks good, feels great, smells terrible. Here's your answer, Jeff. You're a cunt!'

* * *

Skase is facing deportation from Majorca and has lain down in the middle of the road threatening to douse himself in petrol and set himself on fire.

And someone is walking around in circles taking up a collection for him.

'How much have you got so far?' asks an Australian journalist.

'So far? 45 litres.'

*   *   *

John Laws

What's the difference between black and white?
About $1.2 million.

What's black and red all over then white and red
all over?
John Laws's editorials on successive days.

How do you know when John Laws is saying
something he has been paid for?
His lips are moving.

How do you know when John Laws is giving his
unsolicited opinion?
The sun is obscured by a large number of pigs.

How many sides are there to John Laws?
How many would you like?

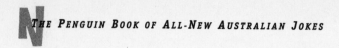

What's the difference between John Laws and the Olympic Games?
The Olympics aren't 100 per cent sold out.

* * *

How many John Howards does it take to change a light bulb?
Change?!?!?!?

ONWARD CHRISTIAN SOLDIERS

OLD AGE

OLYMPIC SPIRIT

OXYMORONS

ONWARD CHRISTIAN SOLDIERS

An American businessman was in Rome, and with only a few days remaining in his trip decided he wanted to see the Pope. He went to the Vatican, and waited in line for a long time. Finally the Pope emerged and proceeded down the line.

The businessman was wearing his finest Armani suit and Italian leather shoes, and was hoping that the Pope would notice him. To his disappointment, however, the Pope went straight past him without so much as a glance.

The businessman was even further dismayed when, a few metres further down the line, the Pope stopped in front of a decrepit local tramp, leant forward and said a few words into the tramp's ear.

Straight afterwards the businessman went up to

the tramp and offered to trade his Armani suit for the tramp's shabby outfit. The tramp readily agreed.

The next day the businessman went back to the Vatican wearing the tramp's gear, and to all appearances looking (and smelling) like a homeless bum. He waited in the line again until the Pope emerged and proceeded down the line. This time the Pope noticed him immediately, came straight towards him, leant forward and whispered in his ear: 'I thought I told you to fuck off!'

✫   ✫   ✫

On the sixth day of creation, God was looking troubled. 'What is it, God?' inquired a sympathetic angel.

'I've got to create the first mother. And the specifications represent a considerable challenge, even for me.'

'What are they?' asked the angel.

'Well, she has to have a kiss that can cure anything from a broken leg to a broken heart. And she must have six pairs of hands.'

'Six pairs of hands?'

'And it's not the hands that are the major problem. It's the three pairs of eyes that a mother must have.'

'On a standard model?'

God nodded. 'Yes, one that sees through walls when she asks "What are you kids doing in there?" (Of course, she already knows.) Another pair in the back of the head so that she sees what she shouldn't ... but what she has to know. And of course the eyes in the front that look at a naughty kid full of understanding and love. Eyes that say all that, and more, without uttering a single word.'

'Lord,' said the angel, touching the hem of his gown, 'go to bed. Get some rest. And tomorrow you can ...'

'I can't,' said God. 'I'm close to creating something much, much closer to myself than man. Already I've one who heals herself when she's sick, who can feed a big family with a couple of dollars of ingredients, who can get a nine-year-old to tidy his room.'

The angel examined the prototype mother very carefully. 'It looks too soft.'

'But tough!' said the Lord proudly. 'You can't imagine what this mother can do and endure.'

'Can it think?'

'Not only can it think, but it can reason. It can compromise. It can teach,' said the creator.

And the angel bent down to run gentle fingers across the cheek of the model of the mother. 'Lord, it's sprung a leak,' she said. 'Perhaps you're trying to put too much into it.'

'That's not a leak,' said God. 'That's a tear.'

'A tear?'

'Yes. The specifications say it's for joy, sadness, pain, loneliness, pride, disappointment.'

'A tear,' echoed the angel. 'God, you're a genius.'

And God, looking faintly puzzled, said: 'I didn't put it there.'

☆   ☆   ☆

Reverend,' said the parishioner, 'I've a problem. My wife keeps falling asleep during your sermons. What should I do?'

'I've an idea,' said the minister. 'Take this hatpin

with you. I've a very good view from the pulpit and will be able to tell you when she's nodding off. So when I motion, you give her a quick jab in the leg with the pin.'

The following Sunday the wife dozed off. Whereupon the preacher put his plan to work. 'And who made the ultimate sacrifice for you?' he asked the congregation, while nodding at the husband. He jabbed his wife with the pin and she cried out in pain: 'Jesus!'

'Yes, you are right. It was Jesus,' said the minister, lifting his hands heavenward.

Soon, the woman nodded off again. Again, the minister responded. 'Who is your redeemer?' he asked the people packing the pews, simultaneously motioning to the husband. 'God!' cried the woman as she was jabbed with the pin.

'Right again! God!' And the minister continued his sermon.

But before long, the woman dozed off again. This time the minister was too excited by his own sermon to notice – and was making gestures that the husband mistook as signals. And just when the minister asked 'And what did Eve say to Adam after she bore him his 99th son?', the woman got the biggest jab of all.

And she shrieked: 'You stick that damn thing in me one more time and I'll break it off and shove it up your arse!'

One day the Lord came to Adam to pass on some news. 'I've got good news and bad news,' the Lord said.

Adam looked at the Lord and said: 'Well, give me the good news first.'

Smiling, the Lord explained: 'I've got two new organs for you. One is called a brain. It will allow you to create new things, solve problems and have intelligent conversations with Eve.'

The Lord continued: 'The other organ I have for you is called a penis. It will give you great physical pleasure and allow you to reproduce your new intelligent life form and populate this planet. Eve will be very happy that you now have this organ to give her children.'

Adam, very excited, exclaimed: 'These are great gifts you have given me. What could possibly be bad news after such great tidings?'

The Lord looked upon Adam and said with great sorrow: 'I've only given you enough blood to use one of them at a time.'

✫　✫　✫

Why God Never Received Tenure at a University

1 Because he had only one major publication.
2 And it was in Hebrew.
3 And it had no cited references.
4 And it wasn't published in a referee journal or even submitted for peer review.
5 And some even doubt he wrote it himself.
6 It may be true that he created the world, but what has he done since?
7 The scientific community had a very tough time trying to replicate his results.
8 He rarely came to class – just told students to read the book.

9 He expelled his first two students for learning.

10 Although there were only ten requirements, most students failed his tests.

11 His office hours were infrequent and usually held on a mountaintop.

A nun is walking through the back streets of Kings Cross when she comes upon a drunk lying in the gutter outside a pub. She stoops down and says: 'You poor man. Don't you know that the demon drink is ruining your life? Come with me to the mission and we'll help you to stop drinking.'

The drunk opens one eye, looks up and says: 'Sister, a little drink now and then isn't so bad. But I'll tell you what I'll do. You come inside and have a drink. Then I'll go with you to the mission.'

The nun agrees, but says: 'I don't want to be seen going into a pub. Could you bring the drink out here?'

'No trubs,' says the drunk.

'And another thing,' says the nun, 'can you put the drink in a coffee cup?'

'No trubs.'

The nun gives him the money, and he goes inside the pub and places the order. 'A whisky for me and a whisky for my friend. But I want you to put it in a coffee cup.'

And the barman says: 'Right. So that nun's out there again?'

*　*　*

There were 500 nuns in the convent. One day after prayers the Mother Superior said: 'One of you has had sex with the priest!' There were 499 cries of 'Oh no!' and one giggle.

'We found the condom,' said the Mother Superior. Again there were 499 cries of 'Oh no!' and one giggle.

'The condom had a hole in it!' There were 499 giggles and one 'Oh no'.

✷ ✷ ✷

God was just about done creating the universe, but he had two extra things left in his bag of creations. So he decided to split them between Adam and Eve. He told the couple that one of the things he had to give away was the ability to stand up while urinating.

'It's a very handy thing,' God told the couple. 'I was wondering if either one of you wanted that ability.'

Adam jumped up and blurted out: 'Oh, give that to me! I'd love to be able to do that! It seems the sort of thing a man should do. Oh please, oh please, let me have that ability ... it'd be so great! When I'm working in the garden or naming the animals, I could just stand there and let it fly. It'd be so cool. I could write my name in the sand! Oh please God, let it be me who you give that gift to, let me stand to pee, oh please!'

On and on he went like an excited little boy who had to pee.

Eve just smiled and told God that if Adam really

wanted it so badly, he should have it. It seemed the sort of thing that would make him really happy so she wouldn't mind if Adam were the one given that ability.

And so Adam was given the ability to urinate while in a vertical position. He was happy, and celebrated by wetting down the bark on the tree nearest him, laughing with delight all the while.

'Fine,' God said, looking into his bag of leftovers. 'What's left here? Ah yes ... multiple orgasms!'

Three Proofs That Jesus Was Jewish

He went into his father's business.

He lived at home until he was 33.

He was sure his mother was a virgin, and his mother was sure he was God.

Three Proofs That Jesus Was Irish

He never got married.

He was always telling stories.

He loved the green pastures.

Three Proofs That Jesus Was Puerto Rican

His first name was Jesus.

He was bilingual.

He was always being harassed by the authorities.

Three Proofs That Jesus Was Italian

He talked with his hands.

He had wine with every meal.

He worked in the building trade.

Three Proofs That Jesus Was Black

He called everyone 'Brother'.

He liked gospel.

He couldn't get a fair trial.

Three Proofs That Jesus Was a Californian

He never cut his hair.

He walked around barefoot.

He started a new religion.

Three Proofs That Jesus Was a Woman

She had to feed a crowd at a moment's notice when there was no food.

She kept trying to get her message across to a bunch of men who just didn't get it.

Even when she was dead, she had to get up because there was more work for her to do.

$$\star \quad \star \quad \star$$

It's over 6000 years since the Creation and things are getting harder and harder for God. There are now six billion human beings and, despite the growing popularity of atheism, materialism and humanism, God is still flat out dealing with the prayers and problems of Christians, Jews and Muslims. In fact, the workload is so enormous that God isn't at all concerned with the continuing popularity of Hinduism and Buddhism, nor with the growing popularity of witchcraft and sundry forms of New Age paganism.

One afternoon he's talking to St Peter. 'Pete, I need a holiday. You know, I haven't rested since the seventh day of Creation. It's just been go, go, go! And talking about going, any suggestions where I might go for a break?'

St Peter thinks and says: 'How about Jupiter? Quite nice this time of year.'

But God says: 'No, too much gravity on Jupiter. It gives me rheumatism.'

St Peter says: 'Okay ... how about Mercury?'

God says: 'God no! Way too hot on Mercury!'

So St Peter says: 'Well, how about going to Earth? I know you keep an eye on all the believers, listening to their prayers. And as well, you hear every falling sparrow. But you actually haven't been to Earth for ages.'

God says: 'You've got to be kidding. I was there 2000 years ago, had an affair with some Jewish girl and they're still talking about it.'

☆　　☆　　☆

A Roman Catholic priest, a Church of England vicar and a rabbi were discussing miracles. The Catholic priest told of a jockey in his congregation who'd been miraculously cured of a bout of haemorrhoids, an ailment that was threatening his career. The vicar told of a woman in his congregation who'd decided to commit suicide and had hurled herself off a tall building, only to change her mind on the way down. 'She prayed to God and, miraculously, he allowed her to land on an awning.'

And the rabbi told how he'd arrived at the synagogue one Saturday morning and discovered a large suitcase sitting on the steps. 'I opened it up and there, lo and behold, was a million dollars. But being the Sabbath I wasn't permitted to touch it. So I prayed for a miracle and, suddenly, it was Wednesday for 100 metres in every direction!'

*   *   *

The Pope was touring Australia and took a couple of days from his itinerary to visit the tropics and the outback. Deep into his visit, his 4WD Popemobile was driving alongside a river when he heard some splashing up ahead.

As he drew close, the Pope observed in the river an Aboriginal man struggling frantically with a crocodile, who had grasped the poor guy in its powerful jaws.

At that moment, from around the riverbend, a speedboat roared into view containing three people – Bruce Ruxton, Arthur Tunstall and Pauline Hanson.

As the speedboat neared the struggling figures, Hanson took aim and fired a harpoon into the crocodile's hide. Then Ruxton and Tunstall pulled the man from the jaws of the crocodile, and, using long clubs, beat the crocodile to death. They bundled the semiconscious man onto the speedboat, as well as the dead croc, and then approached the riverbank.

The Pope was impressed by what he had witnessed, so he went up to greet them.

He said: 'I give you my blessing for your brave actions. I have heard there are some xenophobic people trying to divide Australia's community, but now I can see that your society is a truly enlightened example of racial harmony and could serve as a model for other nations to follow.'

As the Popemobile drove off, Hanson asked the others: 'Who was that?'

Ruxton answered: 'That was His Holiness the

Pope. He is in direct contact with God, and has access to all God's wisdom.'

Hanson: 'Well, he knows fuck-all about crocodile fishing!'

✳   ✳   ✳

A young woman was sitting on her professor's lap while he expounded to her his theories of reincarnation. She said: 'Professor, do you really think I should be sitting on your lap while you expound to me your theories of reincarnation?'

And the professor said: 'Oh, what the hell, we only live once.'

✳   ✳   ✳

In the beginning God created heaven and earth. Quickly he was faced with a class action suit for failure to file an Environmental Impact Statement. He was granted a temporary permit for the project, but was stymied with a Cease and Desist Order for the earthly part. At the ensuing hearing, God was asked why he began his earthly project in the first place. He replied that he just liked to be creative.

Then God said: 'Let there be light.' Officials immediately demanded to know how the light would be made. Would there be strip mining? What about thermal pollution? God explained that the light would come from a huge ball of fire. God was granted provisional permission to make light, assuming that no smoke would result from the ball of fire, that he would obtain a building permit and (to conserve energy) would have the light out half the time. God agreed and said he would call the light 'Day' and the darkness 'Night'. Officials replied that they were not interested in semantics.

God said: 'Let the earth bring forth green herbs and many seeds.' The EPA agreed so long as only native seed was used. Then God said: 'Let the waters bring forth creeping creatures having life, and the fowl that may have flight over the earth.' Officials pointed out that this would require approval from the Ministry for National Parks.

Everything seemed on track until God sought to complete the project in six days. Officials informed him that it would take at least 200 days to review the application and the Environmental Impact Statement. After that there would be a public hearing. Then there would be 10 to 12 months before a judgement.

At this point God created hell.

✯   ✯   ✯

A man walked into the ladies' section of a large department store. He shyly walked up to the woman behind the counter and said: 'I'd like to buy a bra for my wife.'

'What type of bra?' asked the salesperson.

'Type?' inquired the man. 'There's more than one type?'

'Look around,' said the salesperson, as she showed a sea of bras in every shape, size, colour and material. 'Actually, even with all this variety, there are really only three types of bras,' she said.

Confused, the man asked what the types were.

The salesperson replied: 'The Catholic type, the Salvation Army type and the Baptist type. Which one do you need?'

Still confused, he asked: 'What's the difference between them?'

The woman responded: 'It's really quite simple. The Catholic type supports the masses, the Salvation Army type lifts up the fallen, and the Baptist type makes mountains out of molehills.'

*   *   *

A shy gentleman was preparing to board a plane when he heard that the Pope was on the same flight. 'This is exciting,' thought the gentleman. 'I've always been a big fan of the Pope. Perhaps I'll be able to see him in person.'

Imagine his surprise when the Pope sat down in the seat next to him for the flight. However, the gentleman was too shy to speak to the pontiff.

Shortly after takeoff, the Pope began a crossword puzzle. 'This is fantastic,' thought the gentleman. 'I'm really good at crosswords. Perhaps, if the Pope gets stuck, he'll ask me for assistance.'

Almost immediately, the Pope turned to the gentleman and said, 'Excuse me, but do you know a four-letter word referring to a woman that ends in "unt"?'

Only one word leapt to mind. 'My goodness,' thought the gentleman, 'I can't tell the Pope that. There must be another word.'

The gentleman thought for quite a while, then it hit him. Turning to the Pope, the gentleman said: 'I think the word you're looking for is "aunt".'

'Of course!' said the Pope. 'Do you have an eraser?'

*   *   *

A country town was plagued by bats. They were eating all the fruit in the orchards, dangling upside down from the telegraph wires and shitting all over the cars, and their stench filled the classrooms at the local state and Catholic schools. But the problem was worst of all in the churches, where huge numbers of bats had flocked. The Catholic priest was discussing the problem with his Methodist and Presbyterian colleagues.

'I've tried everything,' said the priest. 'Noise.

Spray. Cats. Nothing seems to scare them away.'

The Methodist said: 'Me too. I've got thousands in the belfry. I've even had the church fumigated. But it didn't help.'

And the Presbyterian said: 'I baptised all mine. Made them members of the congregation. Have hardly had any back since.'

☆　　☆　　☆

A little girl was in church with her mother when she started feeling ill. 'Mummy,' she said, 'can we leave now?'

'No,' her mother replied.

'Well, I think I have to throw up!'

'Then go out the front door and around to the back of the church and throw up behind a bush.' In about two minutes the little girl returned to her seat.

'Did you throw up?' her mother asked.

'Yes,' the little girl replied.

'Well, how could you have gone all the way to the back of the church and returned so quickly?'

'I didn't have to go out of the church, Mummy,' the little girl replied. 'They have a box near the front door that says "For the Sick".'

A man had been trying for years to meet the Pope. Finally his wish was granted. When the man approached the Pope he said: 'Your Eminence, I am so happy to be given this chance to speak with you and I would like to tell you a joke before I start.'

The Pope replied: 'Of course, my son. Go ahead and tell your joke.'

The man continued: 'There were these two Polacks and . . .'

The Pope interrupted: 'My son, do you realise that I am Polish?'

'I'm sorry, Your Eminence, I'll speak slower.'

* * *

A local preacher was dissatisfied with the small amount in the collection plates each Sunday. Someone suggested to him that perhaps he might be able to hypnotise the congregation into giving more. 'And just how would I go about doing that?' he asked.

'It's very simple. First you turn up the air-conditioner so that the auditorium is warmer than usual. Then you preach in a monotone. Meanwhile, you dangle a watch on a chain and swing it in a slow arc above the lectern and suggest they put $20 in the collection plate.'

So the very next Sunday, the Reverend did as suggested, and lo and behold the plates were full of $20 notes.

Now, the preacher did not want to take advantage of this technique each and every Sunday, so he waited for a couple of weeks and then tried his mass hypnosis again. Just as the last of the congregation was becoming mesmerised, the chain on the watch broke and the watch hit the lectern with a loud thud. Springs and parts flew everywhere.

'Shit!' exclaimed the pastor.

It took them a week to clean up the church.

A new monk arrives at the monastery. He is assigned to help the other monks in copying the old texts by hand. He notices, however, that they are copying copies, not the original books. So the new monk goes to the head monk and asks him about this. He points out that if there'd been an error in the first copy, that error would be continued in all of the other copies.

The head monk says: 'We have been copying from the copies for centuries, but you make a good point, my son.' So he goes down into the cellar with one of the copies to check it against the original.

Hours later, nobody has seen him. So one of the monks goes downstairs to look for him. He hears sobbing coming from the back of the cellar and finds the old monk leaning over one of the original books, crying. He asks what's wrong.

'The word is "celebrate"!' says the old monk.

A bloke walks into a pub, sits down and orders a beer. And he notices a bloke at the other end of the bar who looks exactly like Jesus.

He whispers to the barman: 'That bloke looks like Jesus.'

And the barman says: 'Yeah, he does, doesn't he? Why don't you ask him?'

So the bloke sidles up to the bearded stranger and says: 'Excuse me, mate. Are you, by any chance, Jesus Christ?'

'As a matter of fact, I am,' comes the reply, in a deep, mellifluous voice.

'No kidding! Well, how about a couple of miracles?'

'If you insist,' says Jesus, rather wearily.

And he walks down the bar to where three blokes are having a bit of a chat. 'Excuse me, gentlemen,' says Jesus. 'I sense that one of you has poor hearing.'

And he reaches out and touches one of the drinkers on the left ear.

'Christ!' the bloke says. 'I can hear again! Perfectly!'

Then the Saviour turns to the second man. 'You've had years of problems with arthritis. It makes it very difficult for you to get off your bar stool.'

'That's right, cobber,' says the second man.

So Jesus touches him lightly on the backside, and instantly, the bloke leaps from the bar stool saying: 'Jesus! I feel bonzer!'

Jesus is just about to touch the third man when the man says: 'Piss off! Don't touch me! I'm on worker's comp!'

✳   ✳   ✳

So Adam asked God for a mate.

'What wantest thou?' the Lord asked.

'Someone tall, blonde. A good cook. A great sense of humour. The works!'

'Verily I say unto you, that will cost you an arm and a leg,' sayeth the Lord.

'Yeah? Then what do I get for a rib?' asked Adam.

The rest is history.

OLD AGE

An old codger went to live in an old people's home, and after his first few days in residence, his son went to check on things. 'Well, Dad, how are you getting on?'

'Son, you'll never believe, but when a nurse bathed me she got hold of my penis and asked me if I'd like some relief,' said Dad with a toothless smile.

A few weeks later the son returned. But this time Dad seemed depressed. 'What's the matter, Dad?'

'Well, I fell in the corridor and a male nurse came up behind me and gave me one,' said the old codger.

'Dad, you have to take the rough with the smooth,' said the son. 'At least the nurse looks after you when you're in the bath.'

'Yes,' replied the old man, 'but I only have a bath once a week. And I fall over twice a day.'

* * *

It's the TV room in a twilight home. Old dears are zzzzing off in front of Bert Newton. Others are staring blankly into space. And one of the few ambulatory denizens, an old lady, walks up to an even older man. She says: 'If you drop your pants, I bet I can tell your exact age.'

So the old man stands on wobbly legs and, with considerable difficulty, drops them.

'You're 83 next week,' she says.

'You're right! Eighty-three next week! But how could you tell that by just looking at me without pants on?'

'That's easy,' she said. 'You told me yesterday.'

* * *

A preacher visits an elderly woman from his congregation. As he sits on the couch he notices a small bowl of peanuts on the coffee table.

'Mind if I have a few?' he asks. 'No, not at all,' the woman replies and pushes the bowl closer.

They chat for an hour and as the preacher stands to leave, he realises that instead of eating just a few peanuts, he has emptied the bowl.

'I'm terribly sorry for eating all the peanuts. I just meant to have a few.'

'That's all right,' the woman replied. 'Ever since I lost my teeth, all I can do is suck off the chocolate.'

☆ ☆ ☆

An old man lay dying in the upstairs bedroom. He was reminiscing on all the things he'd most enjoyed in a long life when, suddenly, he smelt the most wonderfully nostalgic smell. His wife was baking biscuits downstairs! His favourite biscuits!

Slowly, painfully, he dragged himself from the bed, crawled across the room and, despite his great weakness, began to descend the stairs. But he fell and crashed down two flights. Bruised and battered, he crawled into the kitchen and, pulling himself to his knees, saw a tray of freshly baked biscuits on the kitchen table. And he reached up and got a biscuit between his frail, shaking fingers. Whereupon his wife whacked his hand with a spatula.

'Why?' he groaned. 'Why did you do that?'

'Leave them alone. They're for the funeral.'

Mildred and Chester have known each other from childhood but have to wait for Mildred's mother to pass away before they can get married. Finally, when they are both in their nineties, the day comes. Back when they were young there was no hanky-panky before marriage, so Chester and Mildred are both still virgins. Needless to say, Chester is pretty excited on their wedding night, having waited patiently all those years. However, Mildred is very apprehensive as she has developed a heart condition and is going to have to tell Chester they can't have sex.

They sit on the bed and Chester detects a little reluctance on Mildred's part. He thinks she's just shy, so he sends her off to the bathroom to get undressed. When she reappears in her red silk nightie he gets her to sit next to him. Not knowing how to get things started, he pulls down one of her shoulder straps. She blushes as red as her nightie, really concerned about telling Chester of her heart condition.

In the meantime Chester is staring at the first breast he's seen since his own mother's. Gravity having taken its course over some ninety years, it's hanging down to Mildred's belly button. He pulls down the other strap and sees the second breast unroll downards before him. Poor Mildred is beside herself. She has to tell Chester now. So she musters all her courage and says with a quivering voice: 'Chester, I have acute angina.'

Chester says: 'I sure hope so. Your boobs look like hell.'

OLYMPIC SPIRIT

A bloke had bought one ticket to the opening ceremony of the Olympics. It had cost him a fortune but he was thrilled to be there. Oddly enough, there were two empty seats beside him – the only empty seats in the entire stadium. Finally, just as a runner entered the arena carrying the flaming torch, a bloke came bounding down the steps and, squeezing past people's knees, sat in one of the empty seats. 'You just made it in time,' the first bloke said.

'Yeah. It was really hard to get here.'

'And what about the empty seat?'

'That belonged to my wife. She'd really looked forward to today. But unfortunately, she died.'

'So you've decided to leave her seat empty? In her memory? You didn't think of offering the ticket to one of your friends?'

'No point. They're all at her funeral.'

* * *

An Irishman, a Scotsman and an Englishman are trying to get in to see the Olympics. But they don't have any tickets. So the Englishman says: 'I've got an idea.'

He goes to a hardware store, buys a broomstick and walks up to the gate of the stadium. The bloke on the gate says: 'And who the fuck are you?'

He says: 'England. Pole vault.'

'Okay,' says the gateman, 'in you go.'

The Scotsman is inspired. He buys a pizza, eats the pizza, keeps the tray and walks up to the bloke at the gate.

'And who the fuck are you?'

'Scotland. Discus.'

'Okay, in you go.'

It's the Irishman's turn. He goes to the hardware store and buys a roll of barbed wire and walks up to the gateman.

'Ireland. Fencing!'

OXYMORONS

Act naturally
Found missing
Resident alien
Airline food
Good grief
Same difference
Almost exactly
Sanitary landfill
Alone together
Legally drunk
Living death
Small crowd
Business ethics
Soft rock
Butthead
Military intelligence
Childproof

Christian Scientists

Passive aggression

Clearly misunderstood

Peace force

Extinct life

Plastic glasses

Computer security

Political science

Tight slacks

Definite maybe

Pretty ugly

Religious tolerance

Microsoft Works

Business sentiment

Moral war

Clinical strike

Laws of war

Democratic capitalism

Radio Australia

Safe sex

Australian republic

Australian monarchy

Efficient design

Fruitful political discussions
With respect ...
Sincere political position
Honest mistake
Statesman

PEACEKEEPING

PEACEKEEPING

Three Australian soldiers were moving slowly through the jungles of East Timor looking for members of a particularly notorious militia group. As they moved through the jungle they kept whispering to themselves, 'One Australian soldier is worth 500 militia men. One Australian soldier is worth 500 militia men.'

Up ahead there were 1000 militia men waiting in the scrub, rifles at the ready. They could hear the Australians moving towards them, getting closer and closer. And they could hear the murmured words, 'One Australian soldier is worth 500 militia men.'

They sent out a scout so they could see exactly where the Australian troops were ... and he came rushing back saying: 'It's a trap! It's a trap! There's three of them!'

* * *

A newly promoted colonel was setting up a makeshift office in the hills near Dili. He was just getting unpacked when, out of the corner of his eye, he noticed a private with a toolbox coming his way.

Wanting to seem important, he grabbed the phone and said: 'Yes, Prime Minister. Yes, I think it's an excellent plan. Yes, the general has discussed it with me. Yes, you've got my support on it. Thanks for the call. Let's touch base again soon. What's that? I can call you John? Bye!'

'And what can I do for you?' he asks the private.

'Nothing, sir. I'm just here to hook up your phone.'

THE BIG QUESTIONS

Q & A

THE BIG QUESTIONS

Some of Life's Unanswered Questions

Do Lipton employees take coffee breaks?

Do cemetery workers prefer the graveyard shift?

Can atheists get insurance against acts of God?

Should you trust a stockbroker who is married to a travel agent?

Can you be a closet claustrophobic?

If nothing sticks to Teflon, how do they make it stick to the pan?

If the pen is mightier than the sword and a picture is worth a thousand words, how dangerous would a fax be?

What was the best thing before sliced bread?

When it rains, why don't sheep shrink?

What if there were no hypothetical questions?

After eating, do amphibians have to wait an hour to get out of the water?

Why is 'abbreviation' such a long word?

How do 'Don't Walk on the Grass' signs get there?

Before they invented drawing boards, what did they go back to?

If love is blind, why is lingerie so popular?

Could crop circles be the work of a serial killer?

If a word in the dictionary was misspelt, how would you know?

Why do they lock petrol station toilets? Are they afraid someone will clean them?

If the police arrest a mime, do they say he has the right to remain silent?

What keeps glue from sticking to the inside of the bottle?

If Barbie is so popular, why do you have to buy her friends?

How do you tell when you run out of invisible ink?

What's the speed of dark?

Despite the cost of living, have you noticed how popular it remains?

What do you get when you cross the Godfather with a philosopher?
An answer you can't understand.

What's the first question a graduate philosopher asks in his or her first job?
Would you like french fries with that, sir?

The first law of philosophy:
For every philosopher there exists an equal and opposite philosopher.

The second law of philosophy:
They're both wrong.

*　　*　　*

Sherlock Holmes and Dr Watson went on a camping trip. After a good meal and a bottle of wine, they lay down for the night and went to sleep. Some hours later Holmes awoke and nudged his faithful friend. 'Watson, look up at the sky and tell me what you see.'

Watson replied: 'I see millions and millions of stars.'

'So what might one deduce from that?'

Watson pondered for a minute. 'Astronomically, it tells me that there are millions of galaxies and potentially billions of planets. Astrologically, I observe that Saturn is in Leo. Horologically, I deduce that the time is approximately a quarter past three. Theologically, I can see that God is all-powerful, and that we are small and insignificant. Meteorologically, I suspect that we will have a beautiful day tomorrow. What does it tell you?'

Holmes was silent for a minute, then spoke: 'Watson, you moron, some bastard has stolen our tent!!'

★　　★　　★

Is something lost in translation with metrication?

A miss is as good as 1.6 kilometres.

Put your best 0.3 of a metre forward.

Spare the 5.03 metres and spoil the child.

Twenty-eight grams of prevention is worth 453 grams of cure.

Give a man 2.5 centimetres and he'll take 1.6 kilometres.

Peter Piper picked 8.8 litres of pickled pepper.

Q What's the difference between a girlfriend and a wife?

A Twenty kilos.

Q What's the difference between a boyfriend and a husband?

A Forty-five minutes.

Q How can you tell if your wife is dead?

A The sex is the same but the dishes pile up.

Q How can you tell if your husband is dead?

A The sex is the same but you get the remote.

Q Do you know the punishment for bigamy?

A Two mothers-in-law.

Q What's the difference between a terrorist and a Jewish mother?

A You can negotiate with the terrorist.

Q Why do men snore when they lie on their backs?

A Because their balls fall over their arsehole and they vapour-lock.

Q Why did cavemen pull their women around by the hair?

A Because if they pulled them around by their feet, they'd fill up with mud.

Q What's it called when a woman is paralysed from the waist down?

A Marriage.

Q If your wife keeps coming out of the kitchen to nag you, what have you done wrong?

A Made her chain too long.

Q How many men does it take to change a light bulb?

A None. They just sit there in the dark and complain.

Q Why are men and parking spaces alike?

A Because all the good ones are gone and the only ones left are disabled.

Q What have men and floor tiles got in common?

A If you lay them properly the first time, you can walk all over them for life.

Q Why do men want to marry virgins?

A They can't stand criticism.

Q Why is it so hard for women to find men that are sensitive, caring and good-looking?

A Because those men already have boyfriends.

Q What is a man's view of safe sex?

A A padded headboard.

Q How do men sort their laundry?

A 'Filthy' and 'filthy but wearable'.

Q Why do women fake orgasm?

A Because they think men care.

Q Who is the most popular guy at the nudist colony?

A The guy who can carry a cup of coffee in each hand and a dozen doughnuts.

Q Why do men take showers instead of baths?

A Pissing in the bath is disgusting.

Q Who is the most popular girl at the nudist colony?

A The one who can eat the last doughnut.

Q Why does the bride always wear white?

A Because it's good for the dishwasher to match the stove and refrigerator.

Q What is the difference between a battery and a woman?

A A battery has a positive side.

Q Did you hear about the guy who finally figured out women?

A He died laughing before he could tell anybody.

Q How many men does it take to open a beer?

A None. It should be opened by the time she brings it.

Q Why is a laundromat a really bad place to pick up a woman?

A Because a woman who can't afford a washing machine will never be able to support you.

Q Why do women have smaller feet than men?

A So they can stand closer to the kitchen sink.

Q How do you know when a woman is about to say something smart?

A When she starts her sentence with 'A man once told me ...'

Q If your dog is barking at the back door and your wife is yelling at the front door, who do you let in first?

A The dog, of course. At least he'll shut up after you let him in.

Q How do you fix a woman's watch?

A You don't. There's a clock on the oven.

Q What's worse than a male chauvinist pig?

A A woman that won't do as she's told.

Q Why do men die before their wives?

A They want to.

Q What is the difference between a dog and a fox?

A About five drinks.

Q What do you call kids born in whorehouses?

A Brothel sprouts.

Q What do you call a Serbian prostitute?

A Sloberdown Mydickyoubitch.

Q A brunette, a blonde and a redhead are all in third grade. Who has the biggest boobs?

A The blonde, because she's 18.

Q What do you call three dogs and a black bird?

A Spice Girls.

Q What's the difference between a woman and a sheep?

A The sheep doesn't get upset if you screw her sister.

Q How do you turn a fox into an elephant?

A Marry it.

Q What do you get when you cross two black people?

A Your arse kicked.

Q What is the difference between a drug dealer and a hooker?

A A hooker can wash her crack and sell it again.

Q What's the height of conceit?

A Having an orgasm and calling out your own name.

RANDOM THOUGHTS

RECIPES FOR DISASTER

RURAL SECTOR

RANDOM THOUGHTS

Depression is merely anger without enthusiasm.

Drink till she's beautiful, but stop before the wedding.

I'm not cheap, but I'm on special this week.

I almost had a psychic girlfriend, but she left me before we met.

I intend to live forever. So far, so good.

Quantum mechanics. The dreams stuff is made of.

Support bacteria – they're the only culture most people have.

The only substitute for manners: fast reflexes.

When everything is coming your way, you're in the wrong lane.

Ambition is a poor excuse for not having enough sense to be lazy.

Give a man a free hand and he'll run it all over you.

Beauty is in the eye of the beer-holder.

If everything seems to be going well, you've obviously overlooked something.

Dancing is a perpendicular expression of a horizontal desire.

Everyone has a photographic memory. Most don't have film.

Boycott shampoo! Demand real poo!

I used to have an open mind, but my brain kept falling out.

Shin: a device for finding furniture in the dark.

Join the army. Meet interesting people. Kill them.

For sale: Parachute. Only used once. Never opened. Small stain.

I tried sniffing coke, but the ice cubes got stuck in my nose.

Champagne for my real friends, real pain for my sham friends!

RECIPES FOR DISASTER

An Irishman, a Mexican and a One Nation voter were working on the scaffolding of a tall building. They were eating lunch. The Irishman said: 'Corned beef and fucking cabbage. If I get fucking corned beef and cabbage one more time for lunch, I'm going to jump off this building.'

The Mexican opened his lunchbox and exclaimed: 'Burritos again! If I get fucking burritos one more time, I'm going to jump off, too.'

The One Nation voter opened his lunch and said: 'Vegemite again. If I get a Vegemite sandwich one more time, I'm jumping too.'

The next day the Irishman opened his lunchbox, saw fucking corned beef and cabbage and jumped to his death.

The Mexican opened his lunch, saw a burrito and jumped too.

The One Nation voter opened his lunch, saw a Vegemite sandwich and jumped to his death as well.

At the funeral the Irishman's wife was weeping. She said: 'If I'd known how tired he was of corned beef and cabbage I'd never have given it to him again.'

The Mexican's wife, also weeping, said: 'I could have given him tacos or enchiladas. If only I'd known he hated burritos so much.'

Everyone turned and stared at the One Nation voter's wife. 'Hey, don't look at me,' she said. 'The dumb bastard always made his own lunch.'

*　　*　　*

A bloke goes to a restaurant in Surry Hills and orders chicken noodle soup. He starts sipping the soup only to choke on a hair. After gagging for a minute, he calls the waitress. 'There's a hair in this soup!' And he storms out of the restaurant without paying. The waitress watches him cross the street to the Touch of Class, Sydney's most famous brothel.

The waitress is furious at losing her tip. But

even worse, the manager blames her for the incident and announces that he'll dock her wages. When she protests, she gets the sack.

Infuriated, she hurls her apron on the floor and strides over to the brothel to remonstrate with the recalcitrant customer. She crashes into the room and sees the customer performing cunnilingus. 'You wouldn't pay for the chicken noodle soup because you found a hair in it. Now look where your face is!'

The bloke looks up and says: 'And if I find a noodle in here, I won't pay for that either.'

Two cannibals, a father and son, were elected by the tribe to go out and get something to eat. They walked deep into the jungle and waited by a path. Before long, along came a little old man. The son said: 'Ooh Dad, there's one.'

'No,' said the father. 'There's not enough meat on that one to feed even the dogs. We'll just wait.'

A little while later, along came a really fat man.

The son said: 'Hey Dad, he's plenty big enough.'

'No,' the father said. 'We'd all die of a heart attack from the fat in that one. We'll just wait.'

About an hour later, along came an absolutely gorgeous woman. The son said: 'Now, there's nothing wrong with that one, Dad. Let's eat her.'

'No,' said the father. 'We'll not eat her either.'

'Why not?' asked the son.

'Because we're going to take her back alive and eat your mother.'

RURAL SECTOR

In Far North Queensland an old lady in the early stages of Alzheimer's wanders off from the farm. Her daughter, the farmer's wife, is very upset and the farmer, somewhat reluctantly, agrees to mount a search. But not even an Aboriginal tracker can find a trace of her.

Weeks pass until they get a phone call from the owner of a neighbouring property. 'I've got good news and bad news,' he says.

'Well,' says the farmer, 'you'd better give me the bad news first.'

'We've found your wife's mum drowned in a dam.'

'And the good news?'

'Well, there are five enormous yabbies attached to her. Biggest yabbies I've ever seen. What should we do?'

'Look, you keep three of the yabbies and give me the other two. Then toss her back in the dam.'

* * *

A farmer is sitting in a country pub getting well and truly pissed. The barman says: 'Look, I'm grateful for the business, but why are you sitting here on this beautiful day getting drunk?'

'Some things you just can't explain,' said the farmer.

'So what happened that's made you so miserable?'

'Well, if you must know, I was sitting by my cow this morning, quietly milking her, and just as the bucket was about full she kicked it over. With her left leg.'

'That's not so bad. Some things you just can't explain. So then what happened?'

'Well, I took her left leg and tied it to the post with some rope. Then I sat down and continued to milk her. But just as I got the bucket about full she kicked it over with her right leg.'

'Again? So what did you do?'

'I took her right leg and tied it to the post on the right.'

'And then what?'

'Then I sat back down and continued milking her. And just as I got the bucket about full, she knocked it over with her tail.'

'You must have been pretty upset! Some things you just can't explain. So what did you do?'

'Well, I didn't have any more rope. So I took the belt out of my trousers and tied her tail to the rafter. At that moment my pants fell down and my wife walked in.'

☆ ☆ ☆

A couple go to Malcolm Fraser's last bull sale at Nareen. The auctioneer begins extolling the virtues of the first bull. 'A fine specimen! This bull reproduced 60 times last year.' The wife nudges her husband in the ribs and says: 'See! That's five times a month.'

Now the second bull is under the hammer.

'Another fine specimen. This fine brahman reproduced 120 times last year.' Again the wife nudges the husband. 'What do you say to that?'

Now a third bull is up for sale. 'This fine beast,' says the auctioneer, 'reproduced 365 times last year.' And the wife almost yells at her husband: 'That's once a day! Every day of the year!'

And the husband snarls: 'Yeah, once a day! Very impressive! But ask Malcolm Fraser if they were all with the same cow!'

S

SCIENTIFIC INQUIRY

SELF-HELP

SHOP TILL YOU DROP

SPORTS REPORT

SCIENTIFIC INQUIRY

A scientist was successful in cloning himself. He was asked to speak at a national convention of cloning scientists. The meeting room was located on the 45th floor of a New York skyscraper.

The scientist arrived with his clone and proceeded to the podium. The clone sat at the end of the head table. The scientist began his speech intending to pay tribute to advances in the field of modern biology.

'My fellow scientists,' he began. But before he could utter another word, the clone sprang to his feet and shouted out: 'He's an ARSEHOLE!' The crowd began to murmur as the scientist commanded the clone to 'sit down and shut up'.

Apologising for the interruption, the scientist began again: 'My fellow scientists ...' Again the clone sprang to his feet and yelled: 'The dumb ARSE couldn't produce a copy on a Xerox. He's a fraudulent SON-OF-A-BITCH!'

Incensed, the scientist rushed to the clone, grabbed him and threw him out of the window. The crowd gasped and security guards rushed into the room. A short while later New York's finest arrived and heard about the events that had transpired.

The police chief said to the scientist: 'We are going to have to arrest you.'

The scientist replied: 'For what? I have committed no crime. What fell from the window was a clone, not a person.'

The attending scientists nodded in agreement. 'Well,' retorted the police chief. 'We cannot let this heinous act go unchallenged.'

The police chief thought for a moment and then ordered the scientist be held for 'Making an obscene clone fall . . .'

A man is driving down a country road when he spots a farmer standing in the middle of a huge field of grass. He pulls his car over to the side of the road and notices that the farmer is just standing there, doing nothing, looking at nothing.

The man gets out of his car, walks all the way out to the farmer and asks him: 'Ah, excuse me mate, but what are you doing?'

The farmer replies: 'I'm trying to win a Nobel Prize.'

'How?' asks the man, puzzled.

'Well, I heard they give Nobel Prizes to people who are out standing in their field.'

SELF-HELP

I have the power to channel my imagination into ever-soaring levels of suspicion and paranoia.

I assume full responsibility for my actions, except the ones that are someone else's fault.

I no longer need to punish, deceive or compromise myself. Unless, of course, I want to stay employed.

In some cultures what I do would be considered normal.

Having control over myself is nearly as good as having control over others.

I can change any thought that hurts into a reality that hurts even more.

I honour my personality flaws, for without them I would have no personality at all.

I need not suffer in silence while I can still moan, whimper and complain.

When someone hurts me, forgiveness is cheaper than a lawsuit. But not nearly as gratifying.

The first step is to say nice things about myself. The second, to do nice things for myself. The third, to find someone to buy me nice things.

I am at one with my duality.

I will strive to live each day as if it were my 50th birthday.

Only a lack of imagination saves me from immobilising myself with imaginary fears.

False hope is nicer than no hope at all.

A good scapegoat is nearly as welcome as a solution to the problem.

Just for today, I will not sit in my living room all day watching TV. Instead I will move the TV into my bedroom.

Why should I waste my time reliving the past when I can spend it worrying about the future?

I am learning that criticism is not nearly as effective as sabotage.

The next time the universe knocks on my door, I will pretend I am not home.

I am willing to make the mistakes if someone else is willing to learn from them.

SHOP TILL YOU DROP

Tired of constantly being broke, and stuck in an unhappy marriage, a young husband decided to solve both problems by taking out a large insurance policy on his wife (with himself as the beneficiary) and arranging to have her killed.

A 'friend of a friend' put him in touch with a nefarious underworld figure who went by the name of Artie. Artie explained to the husband that the going price for snuffing out a spouse was $5000.

The husband said he was willing to pay that amount, but that he wouldn't have any cash on hand until he could collect his wife's insurance money.

Artie insisted on being paid *something* up front. The man opened his wallet and displayed a single dollar coin that rested inside. Artie sighed, rolled his eyes, and reluctantly agreed to accept the dollar as down payment for the dirty deed.

A few days later, Artie followed the man's wife to the local Safeway supermarket. There he surprised her in the produce department, and proceeded to strangle her with gloved hands.

As the poor unsuspecting woman drew her last breath and slumped to the floor, the manager of the produce department stumbled unexpectedly onto the scene. Unwilling to leave any witnesses behind, Artie had no choice but to strangle the produce manager as well.

Unknown to Artie, the entire proceedings were captured by hidden cameras and observed by the store's security guard, who immediately called the police. Artie was caught and arrested before he could leave the store.

Under intense questioning at the police station, Artie revealed the sordid plan, including his financial arrangements with the hapless husband.

And that's why, the next day in the newspaper, the headline declared: 'Artie chokes two for a dollar at Safeway'.

Deakin University and Coles-Myer recently signed an agreement to establish a degree course. Within hours the following document, detailing 'Recommended Electives' for the undergraduates, had appeared on the Internet under the heading:

Deakinstructing the Coles New World Order

- Introduction to check-out procedures – Money, culture and consumption
- Advanced check-out procedures – Money, culture and more consumption
- Zen and the art of trolley maintenance – An exploration of hegemony, conspicuous consumption and globalisation
- Daytime trolley rage – Gender, class and deviance studies in dysfunctionality
- Trolley rage after dark – Australian subcultures and the nocturnal paradigm
- Calling for a price check – The semiotics of mass communication
- Fundamentals of customer service – Oxymorons in the new millennium

- Basic stocktaking – Ethics, responsibility and how to shop cheaply
- Introduction to store surveillance – Screenwriting for a fly-on-the-wall documentary
- Advanced store surveillance – Text and subtext in virtual realities
- Computerised stock control – The computer hacker as urban warrior
- Introduction to visual merchandising – Representation of self and other
- Advanced visual merchandising – Windows 2000 and the need for transparency
- Virtual visual merchandising – Job opportunities for the post-package employee
- Identifying the Red Spot Special – Uniformity and difference in post-urban environments
- Managing the deli – Stereotypes and the myth of multiculturalism
- Frozen-food fundamentals – Cryogenics and the ethics of sustainability
- The Christmas store – Towards a homogeneous monoculture

- The Easter store – The eggsistential crisis of consumption
- Home improvements for senior executives – Sociology of corruption, reading case studies
- Stress management for senior executives – Golf, politics and the bunker mentality

✴   ✴   ✴

A bloke walks into a hot bread shop. Apart from the proprietor, it is absolutely empty.

'Can I have a loaf of bread, please?'

'Wait your turn. Back to the end of the queue!'

The customer looks around. There's nobody else there. Nonetheless he goes outside the shop, waits a few seconds, and then returns.

'Now can I have a loaf of bread?'

And the shopkeeper says: 'Of course.' When he turns around to get the bread, the customer belts him over the head.

The shopkeeper turns around and says: 'Who did that?'

And the customer says: 'With all this crowd, it's hard to say!'

✱   ✱   ✱

A bloke goes up to the proprietor of an ice-cream parlour and, seeing there's no one else there, asks the proprietor somewhat diffidently: 'Can you make up any flavour ice-cream?'

'Of course. What do you want?'

The curious customer, looking around in case of eavesdroppers, says: 'Well, I bet you quids you can't make me a litre of cunt-flavoured ice-cream.'

The proprietor replies: 'A most unusual request, but not beyond my expertise. Though it will, of course, require some delicacy in the harvesting of the flavour.'

The customer can hardly contain himself. 'Great news, mate. Now, when could I hope to pick up this much-desired litre of cunt-flavoured ice-cream?'

'Well, it'll be ready in a week, but it'll cost you big bucks.'

The customer replied: 'No problem. Please go ahead.'

Next week he takes delivery of the ice-cream, pays the proprietor and leaves, anxious to try the treat.

Next day he returns to the parlour. The proprietor inquires: 'Were you pleased with the ice-cream?'

Customer: 'Well, I was thrilled with my first taste of cunt-flavoured ice-cream. But at the end I noticed an unusual flavour creeping in. It was a taste like shit. Can you explain why this should be?'

The proprietor, unfazed, announces to the bewildered customer: 'It's easy, mate. You took too big a lick.'

SPORTS REPORT

Two teams are preparing for a game of cricket. But one team is without an opening bat.

'Where's Bill?'

'He's sick. Couldn't make it. It's okay, I've got a horse that bats.'

'You've got a what?'

'I've got a horse that's a very good batsman.'

'Okay, go get him.'

They start the game and the horse is absolutely brilliant. Hits six after six after six.

Now it's time to change overs, and the second batsman gives the ball a great clout and starts running. But the horse just stands there.

So the batsman asks the horse: 'Why didn't you run?'

'I'm a batsman. If I could run I'd be at fucking Randwick!'

It was late at night in Thredbo and three blokes – total strangers – arrived at the reception desk seeking accommodation.

'Sorry,' said the receptionist, 'but we've only got one room. You'd have to share.' The three men seemed agitated. 'But don't worry, it's only for one night. There'll be plenty of rooms in the morning.'

'Well, if it's just for one night,' the blokes said, and headed for the lift. And they finished up sharing one large bed.

The next morning the bloke on the far right said: 'I had a really odd dream last night. I kept dreaming that I was wanking like a chimpanzee, but I couldn't feel my hand.'

'That's really strange,' said the bloke on the far left. 'I had exactly the same dream.'

And the man in the middle said: 'Talking about strange dreams, I dreamt that I was out skiing.'

A young guy out on the town with his mates spies the girl of his dreams across the dance floor. Having admired her from afar, he plucks up the courage to talk to her. Everything goes better than expected and she agrees to accompany him on a date the following Saturday evening.

Saturday night arrives and the guy comes to her house laden with flowers and chocolates. To his amazement she answers the door in nothing but a towel.

'I'm sorry,' she exclaims, 'I'm running a bit late. Please come in and I'll introduce you to my parents, who will entertain you while I finish getting dressed. I should warn you, however, that they are both deaf mutes.' With that she ushers him into the living room, introduces him to her parents and promptly disappears. As you can imagine this is a little uncomfortable, as both parents are completely silent.

Dad is sitting in his armchair watching the soccer, and Mum is busy knitting. After about ten minutes of complete silence, Mum suddenly jumps from her chair, pulls up her skirt, pulls down her knickers and pours a glass of water over her arse.

Just as suddenly Dad launches himself across the room, bends her over the couch and takes her from behind. He then sits back down in his chair and places a matchstick under each eyelid. The room is plunged back into eerie silence and the young man is shocked into disbelief.

After a further ten minutes the mother again rises from her chair, pulls up her skirt, pulls down her pants and throws a glass of water over her arse. Dad leaps up, gives her one from behind and places two more matchsticks under his eyelids.

No sooner have they concluded this strange behaviour than the daughter returns fully dressed, ready for their date. The evening is a complete disaster, with the young man distracted by the goings-on in the living room.

At the end of the evening the girl asks: 'What's the matter? Have I done something wrong?'

'It's not you,' replied her date. 'It's just that the strangest thing happened while I was waiting for you and I am still a bit shocked.'

After she pleads with him to explain in more detail, the young man reluctantly recounts the story.

'Well, first your mother jumps from her chair and lifts up her skirt. She then pulls down her pants and throws a glass of water over her behind.'

'I see,' says the girl. 'What happened then?'

'Well, as if that isn't enough your father races from his chair, leans Mum over the couch and does her from behind. He then sits back down and places a matchstick under each eyelid.'

'Oh, is that all?' replies the girl.

The young man can't believe the casual response to this weird practice. She says: 'It's easily explained. Mum was simply saying, "Are you going to get this arsehole a drink?" and Dad was replying, "No, fuck him. I'm watching the match".'

T

Thespian Tendencies
The Truth, the whole truth &
nothing but the truth

THESPIAN TENDENCIES

An elderly chorus boy is given a small part in a play. He has to walk onto the stage, sit down and say: 'Well, here I am.' But at rehearsal his performance is unsatisfactory.

'NO!' bellowed the director. 'Try it again.'

So he tried it again. 'Well, here I am.'

'Do it once more. But this time, come on like a man!'

'My goodness,' simpered the actor. 'For $50 a week he wants me to do character parts.'

THE TRUTH, THE WHOLE TRUTH & NOTHING BUT THE TRUTH

A car accident. Both cars are badly smashed but neither driver is hurt.

They crawl out of their cars, brush themselves down and agree that they're very, very lucky not to have been killed.

'This must be a sign from God that we should be friends and live together in peace the rest of our days,' said one of the motorists, a not unattractive woman.

The other driver, a man, replied: 'I agree with you completely. This must be a sign from God.'

And the woman said: 'And look at this – another miracle. Though my car is completely demolished, this bottle of Grange Hermitage didn't break. Surely the Lord wants us to drink this wine and celebrate our good fortune.' So she handed the bottle to the man, who, nodding his head in agreement, popped the cork and took a few big swigs.

Then he handed the bottle back to the woman, who graciously declined it. 'No, you can have the rest.'

The bloke said: 'Are you sure you don't want any?'

And she replied: 'No. I think I'll just wait for the police.'

WHY DID THE CHICKEN CROSS THE ROAD?

WORDS OF WISDOM

WHY DID THE CHICKEN CROSS THE ROAD?

A bloke was driving down the Hume Highway when he swerved to avoid hitting a rabbit. But the bunny jumped the wrong way and was skittled.

Being a sensitive bloke as well as an animal lover, the driver pulled over to the side and sadly observed that the bunny was a goner. And he began to cry.

A woman drove by, and seeing the man weeping at the side of the road, pulled over. She wound down the window and asked: 'What's wrong?'

'I feel just awful. I accidentally killed this rabbit.'

The woman told him not to worry. She knew exactly what to do. She opened her glove box, pulled out a spray can, walked over to the dead rabbit and gave the corpse a long squirt.

Whereupon the rabbit came to life, jumped up, waved its paw at the two humans and hopped down the road. It ran a little further, stopped, turned around again and gave another wave. And it kept repeating this, over and over again. It would run, stop, turn and wave.

The bloke was astonished. 'What's in the spray can?'

The woman rotated the can so that the bloke could read the label: HARE SPRAY. RESTORES LIFE TO DEAD HARE. ADDS PERMANENT WAVE.

☆ ☆ ☆

Why did the chicken cross the road?

Sir Edmund Hillary:
Because it's there.

Pauline Hanson:
To steal a job from a decent, hard-working Australian.

John Locke:
Because he was exercising his natural right of liberty.

Albert Camus:
It doesn't matter; the chicken's actions have no meaning except to him.

Emily Dickinson:
Because it could not stop for death.

Fox Mulder:
It was a government conspiracy.

Sigmund Freud:
The fact that you thought that the chicken crossed the road reveals your underlying sexual insecurity.

Richard Nixon:
The chicken did not cross the road. I repeat, the chicken did not cross the road.

Oliver Stone:
The question is not 'Why did the chicken cross the road?' but rather 'Who was crossing the road at the same time whom we overlooked in our haste to observe the chicken crossing?'

The Pope:
That is only for God to know.

Jerry Seinfeld:
Why does anyone cross a road? I mean, why doesn't anyone ever think to ask what the heck this chicken was doing walking around all over the place anyway?

Louis Farrakhan:
The road, you will see, represents the black man. The chicken crossed the 'black man' in order to trample him and keep him down.

Martin Luther King Jr:
I envisage a world where all chickens will be free to cross roads without having their motives called into question.

Immanuel Kant:
The chicken, being an autonomous being, chose to cross the road of his own free will.

Grandpa:
In my day, we didn't ask why the chicken crossed the road. Someone told us that the chicken had crossed the road, and that was good enough for us.

Erich Maria Remarque:
The chicken crossed the road because after his experience with war, he no longer felt at home in his home.

Bill Gates:
I have just released the new Chicken 2000, which will both cross roads *and* balance your cheque book, though when it divides 3 by 2 it gets 1.4999999999.

M.C. Escher:
That depends which plane of reality the chicken was on at the time.

George Orwell:
Because the government had fooled him into thinking that he was crossing the road of his own free will, when he was really only serving their interests.

Colonel Sanders:
I missed one?

Pyrrhon the sceptic:
What road?

Buddha:
If you ask this question, you deny your own chicken nature.

WORDS OF WISDOM

From a noticeboard outside the Ampol service station at Lismore:

I OWE
I OWE
IT'S OFF TO WORK I GO

* * *

For Those Who Take Life Seriously

Save the whales. Collect the whole set.

A day without sunshine is, like, night.

On the other hand, you have different fingers.

I just got lost in thought. It was unfamiliar territory.

Forty-two point seven per cent of all statistics are made up on the spot.

Ninety-nine per cent of lawyers give the rest a bad name.

I feel like I'm diagonally parked in a parallel universe.

You have the right to remain silent. Anything you say will be misquoted, then used against you.

I wonder how much deeper the ocean would be without sponges.

Honk if you love peace and quiet.

Remember: half the people you know are below average.

Nothing is foolproof to a talented fool.

Atheism is a non-prophet organisation.

The early bird may get the worm, but the second mouse gets the cheese.

I drive way too fast to worry about cholesterol.

Borrow money from a pessimist: he doesn't expect to be repaid.

My mind is like a steel trap: rusty and illegal in all states.

If at first you don't succeed, destroy all evidence that you tried.

A conclusion is the place where you got tired of thinking.

Experience is something you don't get until just after you need it.

For every action there is an equal and opposite criticism.

Bills travel through the mail at twice the speed of cheques.

Never do card tricks for the group you play poker with.

No one is listening until you make a mistake.

Success always occurs in private and failure in full view.

The colder the X-ray table, the more of your body is required on it.

The hardness of butter is directly proportional to the softness of bread.

The severity of the itch is inversely proportional to the ability to reach it.

To steal ideas from one person is plagiarism; to steal from many is research.

To succeed in politics, it is often necessary to rise above your principles.

Monday is an awful way to spend one-seventh of your life.

You never really learn to swear until you learn to drive.

Two wrongs are only the beginning.

The problem with the gene pool is that there is no lifeguard.

The sooner you fall behind the more time you'll have to catch up.

A clear conscience is usually a sign of a bad memory.

Get a new car for your spouse: it'll be a great trade!

Plan to be spontaneous.

Always try to be modest and proud of it!

If you think nobody cares, try missing a couple of payments.

How many of you believe in telekinesis? Raise my hand ...

Love may be blind, but marriage is the real eye-opener.

If at first you don't succeed, then skydiving isn't for you.

He who hesitates is probably right.

Everybody repeat after me: 'We are all individuals.'

INDEX

A

Aboriginal Australians 339
  and the Pope 376–8
Adam, and God 367–8, 371–2
African roulette 267–8
African tribes, and the
  professor 339–40
African-Americans 338–9,
  346–7
American businessman 242–4
  and the Pope 362–3
American soldier, and the
  Englishwoman 337–8
appetite, and Viagra 273–4
Australian soldiers
  and East Timorese militia
    400
  and the telephone 401
Australians
  and New Zealanders 12–13
  in Japan 202–3
aviation 18
Azaria 19–20

B

baby seals 34
ball sports 292

bank customers 346
barman, and the lemon juice
  52–3
bats 382–3
bears, in bars 51
beer, prayer for 54–5
beer nuts 37–8
blokes
  and the flavoured ice-cream
    443–4
  and the hot bread shop
    442–3
  reasons to be a bloke 148–9
  rednecks 149–51
  see also men
blondes 57–8, 63
  and alligator shoes 62–3
  and boating 60
  and golf 165–6, 178–9
  and plane trips 61–2, 63–4
  and St Peter 237–8
  and sex 58–9
  and the auction 58
  and the fire brigade 56
  and the Tax Department 57
  and the TV salesman 59–60
  and vending machines 57
  losing weight 56

boating, and blondes 60
boss, and working
    relationships 82–4
boyfriend, and the gift 325–6
bras 203, 380–1
breakfast 34
breathalyser 35
broken engagement 258
brothels 16, 424–5
Brown, Divine 355–6
brunettes 65–6
bulls 429–30
bumper stickers 67–74
buses 196
business advice 75–7, 242–4

C

caddies 164–5, 197, 205–6
camels 112–13
cancer 321
cannibals 425–6
car accident 453–4
castration 317–18
cat, and St Peter 238–9
Catholics, and children 331
changing a light bulb
    298–310
chicken
    and the egg 114–15
    why did the chicken cross
        the road? 457–61
children
    and Catholics 331
    and golf 166–7

and sickness 382–3
and the facts of life 32–3
and the whole truth 39
at school 31–2
before having 22–5
lost child 29
masturbation 33
playing 27
reality and theory 26–7
Chinese, and Greek 329
Chinese sex therapist 312–13
Christmas
    e-mail version '12 days of
        Xmas' 99–104
    economic rationalism '12
        days of Xmas' 94–7
    politically correct '12 days
        of Xmas' 97–9
Christmas party 136–7
Cinderella 140–1
Clinton, Bill 216–17, 218,
    221–4, 229
    and God 212–13
    and Hillary 212, 216,
        217–18, 232–3
    and Jerry Falwell 218
    and Ken Starr 225
    and Monica 224
    and protection 217
    and Saddam Hussein
        214–16, 221
    and sex 213, 214, 224
    and the box under the bed
        232–3
    and the horse's arse 228–9

and the ladies' pants 219
and White House ghosts
233–4
compared with Nixon
225–6
in the Land of Oz 216
my favourite things 226–8
video, compared with
Titanic video 229–31
see also White House
Clinton, Chelsea 219–20,
223
Clinton, Hillary 212, 216,
217–18, 222, 232–3
clones 432–3
cockroaches, and light bulbs
299
Coles-Myer 440–2
computers
and gender 287–9
jargon 285–6
Confucius sayings 348–9
constipation 314–15
consultants 137
contraception 250–1
cows 113, 429–30
crabs and lobsters 109–10
cricket, and the horse 445
cunnilingus 249, 424–5

D

Dad & Dave & Mabel
and the cheque 122–3
and the doctor 122

at Notre Dame cathedral
124
at the dance 126–7
at the fancy dress party
127–8
at the races 125
broke 124
deaf mutes 447–9
Deakin University 440–2
Death Row, and hiccups
296–7
depression 318
desert island 340–2
Di, Princess 353, 354
dingoes, and the shoes
107–8
divorce 310–11, 339
doctors 313–14
and castration 317–18
and God 313
and good/bad news 325
and the blue testicle 323–5
and the marshmallow
322–3
and voluptuous women
319–20
see also gynaecologists;
psychiatrists
dogs
and cats 117–18
and light bulbs 298–9
and restaurants 48–9
philosophy 118–19
drama rehearsal 452
drinking, and police 35

drunks 42
  and golf 176–7, 194
  and the confessional 47
  and the Good Samaritan
    49–50
  and the nun 369–70
  in the groove 50
  on marriage 48
  pissing 47
ducks, and peanuts 46

E

economic hardship 259–60
economic rationalism, and
  Christmas 94–7
elderly couple 272–3, 306–7,
  391–3
elderly golfers 167, 189
elderly men
  and exact age 390
  and the biscuits 391–2
  and the nursing home
    389–90
elderly women
  and the preacher 390–1
  lost on the farm 427–8
elephants 112, 114
employment
  and downsizing 130
  job placement 135–6
  when caught sleeping at the
    desk 131
  see also office life

F

facelift, and looking younger
  262–3
fairy stories
  Cinderella 140–1
  Mickey Mouse 142
  Pinocchio 140
  Snow White 142
Falwell, Jerry 218
family court judge 310
farmers
  and the elderly lady 427–8
  and the Nobel Prize 433–4
  and the things you can't
    explain 428–9
first date 447–9
flies, and light bulbs 300
football 16
Fraser, Malcolm 429–30
fur coat 157

G

Gates, Bill
  and Divine Brown 355–6
  and God 212–13
gays 254–5
gender 146–8
  and computers 287–9
  great reasons for being a
    bloke 148–9
  his and her stories 152–3
  impressing a woman 155–6
  men on women 154–5

rednecks 149–51
seminars for women
    (presented by men)
    157–9
women on men 153–4, 157
see also men; women
general, and the undone fly
    256–7
genetic engineering 17, 105
genies
    and the bridge 153–4
    and the lifeboat 39–40
    and the suburban house
        282–4
Gingrich, Newt 216
glass eye 278–9
God
    Adam and good/bad news
        367–8
    Adam and the rib 388
    Adam and urination 371–2
    and Bill Gates 212–13
    and men dominated by
        women 240
    and mothers 363–5
    and the doctor 313
    and the earthly project
        378–80
    and the holiday destination
        374–5
    and university 368–9
gold prospector, and St Peter
    236
golf
    and blind golfers 192–3

and lovemaking 204–5
and marriage 186, 197–8
and Mother Nature 182–3
and St Peter 172–3, 189–90,
    206–7, 208–9
and sex 193, 198
and skydiving 188
and the arrogant American
    164–5
and the Aussie in Japan
    202–3
and the blonde 165–6,
    178–9
and the bra 203
and the bus 196
and the caddy 164–5, 197,
    205–6
and the call of nature
    162–3, 179, 184
and the drunk golfer
    176–7, 194
and the elderly couple 189
and the elderly golfer 167
and the felled player 208,
    209
and the green slime 174–5
and the headaches 169–72
and the heart attack 185
and the international
    executives 198–9
and the Jewish businessman
    173–5
and the lucky frog 190–1
and the mental patient
    193–4

and the new car 187–8
and the new lady golfer 176
and the physiotherapist
    195
and the pink golf ball
    201–2
and the Pope 180–2
and the wives 163–4, 180,
    183, 200–1, 205
and the young brothers
    166–7
and the young executive
    168
and the young women 186
gravelly lie 175
hooker 184–5
playing through 196
sounds dirty! 178
water hazard 168–9
with husband and wife
    177–8
Gore, Al 212–13, 217–18, 222
Grant, Hugh 355–6
green slime 174–5
gynaecologist 319–20

H

hard times 259–60
headaches 169–72
high finance 242–4
higher education
    and God's lack of tenure
        368–9

language class 245
life after university 246–8
Hinkley, John 231–2
hippos 115
Holmes, Sherlock 407–8
honeymooners 266
horse, and cricket 445
hot bread shop 442–3
Howard, John 360
husbands
    and the hired killer 438–9
    missing 308
    previous 253–4
    see also marriage; men
Hussein, Saddam, and Bill
    Clinton 214–16, 221
hypnosis 384–5

I

information systems
    acronyms 285–6
    computer jargon 286–7
    computers and gender
        287–9
international executives
    198–9
interstate train 250–1
interviewees 77–8
Irish wedding 309–10
Irishman
    and free sex 334–5
    and his brothers 53–4
    and Mother Teresa 331

and nostalgia 332
and the olives 42–3
and the race 330
and the Red Indian 335–6
Mexican and One Nation
    voter 423–4
Pom and a Scot 330, 333,
    395
Italian funeral 328
Italian spelling 328

J

Jackson, Michael 352–3
Jehovah, and the money 344
Jesus
    and miracles 386–8
    cultural origins 372–4
Jewish boy 347–8
Jewish businessman 173–4
Jewish man
    and Lotto 343–4
    and the bank 346
Jewish women, and getting
    smarter 345
job placement 135–6
jockeys, and race tips 263–4
John, Elton 354

K

Kennedy, Teddy 223
Kennett, Jeff, and the terrible
    smell 356–8

Kermit the Frog 115, 116
koala, and the prostitute
    264–5

L

Laws, John 75–7, 359–60
lawyers
    and St Peter 241
    and sex 253–4
    and the pathologist 296
letter of recommendation
    84–5
Lewinsky, Monica 224, 229,
    347
lifeboat wish, and genies
    39–40
lift antics 85–8
light bulbs, changing 298–302
limericks 16–17
linguistics 245
Little Teddy 25–6
Lone Ranger, and Tonto 43–5
loneliness, and the millipede
    110–11
looking younger 262–3
Lord *see* God
lost luggage 336
Lotto winner 343–4
lunch 423–4

M

McCartney, Paul 356
McEnroe, John 224

Mabel *see* Dad & Dave &
  Mabel
mad cow disease 113
magic watch 255
marriage 305–6
  and golf 186, 197–8
  and missing husband 308
  and winning the lottery
    305
married couple
  and the dildo 278
  and the skin graft 307–8
married woman, and the
  previous husbands 253–4
Martians and sex 276–8
masturbation 33, 140
maths class 245–6
medical diagnosis 315–17
medicine man 315
Melbourne Uni students, and
  light bulbs 301
men
  and enjoyment of sex
    255–6
  and light bulbs 299
  and women 409–17
  impressing 156
  on women 154–5
  see also blokes
mermaid, and sex 142–4
metrication 408
Mexican fisherman 242–4
Michael, George 352
Mickey Mouse 142

Microsoft programmers, and
  light bulbs 298
midgets 354–5
millipede 110–11
miracles
  and Jesus 386–8
  and religious leaders 375–6
monkeys 40–2
monks, copying old texts 385
mosquitoes 58, 112
mothers 363–5
multiculturalism 328–49

N

naked woman, and taxi driver
  257–8
neighbourhood dispute
  108–9
New Jersey people, and light
  bulbs 302
New Zealanders
  and Aussies 12–13
  and sheep 15
  and ventriloquist 13–14
Nicklaus, Jack 180–2, 204–5
nightclubs, and ties 38
Nixon, Richard 225–6
Nobel Prize 433–4
nudist club 254–5
nun
  and sex 370
  and the drunk 369–70

O

office gags 78–82
office graffiti 133–5
office life 82–4
    downsizing 130
    inspiration for staff 131
    when caught sleeping at the
        desk 131
old age 389–93
Olympic Games
    getting in without tickets
        395
    opening ceremony tickets
        394
oral sex 272, 280
orgasm 258–9
Oxford Street straight men,
    and light bulbs 301
oxymorons 396–8

P

Packer, James 75–7
parenting 22–5
parishioner
    and the minister 365–7
    and the sick child 383–4
parrots 116–17
Parton, Dolly 222
pathologist, and lawyers 296
peanut in the ear 265–6
penis 159–61, 322–3
Penis Van Lesbian 274–6

pharmacist 322
philosophy 406–7
physiotherapist 195
pickle factory 132
Pinocchio 140
plane trips, and blondes 61–2,
    63–4
police
    and drinking 35
    and the car accident 453–4
Pope
    and golf 180–2
    and the American
        businessman 362–3
    and the crocodile 376–8
    and the crossword puzzle
        381–2
    and the joke 384
prawns 105–7
prayer for beer 54–5
pregnancy, shooting during
    28
prison, versus work 88–90
professor
    and reincarnation 378
    and the African tribes
        339–40
prostitutes 259
    and the koala 264–5
psychiatrists 267, 320–1
pub stories 36–8, 39, 40–3, 45,
    50–4, 330

Q

Quayle, Dan 216
questions
  and answers 409–17
  unanswerable 404–6

R

rabbit, and the accident 456–7
race tips 263–4
random thoughts 420–2
Reagan, Ronald and Nancy
  231–2
reality, and theory 26–7
recreational preferences 292
rednecks 149–51
Reeve, Christopher 352
religious leaders
  and hypnosis 384–5
  and miracles 375–6
  and the bats 382–3
  and the elderly woman
    390–1
  and the parishioner 365–7
  copying old texts 386
republic 17
restaurants
  and dogs 48–9
  and the soup 424–5
Richardson, Graham 75–7

S

saving money 259–60
scientist, and the clone 432–3

self-conscious 77–8
self-help 435–7
sex 146–8, 269
  and Bill Clinton 213, 214,
    224
  and blondes 58–9
  and golf 193, 198
  and the *Lusitania* 249
  and the mermaid 142–4
  and the nun 370
  and the statue 249–50
  and wives 252–3
  Chinese style 269–71
  enjoyment of 255–6
  on Mars 276–8
  Tarzan and Jane 260–1
  women and the husbands
    251–2, 253–4
sex education 32–3
sheep, sex with 15
showbiz 274–6
Simpson, O.J. 352
Skase, Bill 358
ski lodge antics 446
snail salesman 108
Snow White 142
speeding ticket 327
spell checker 90–2
sperm 261
St Peter
  and golf 172–3, 189–90,
    206–7, 208–9
  and Princess Di 353
  and the blondes 237–8
  and the cat 238–9

and the gold prospector 236
and the two blokes 235
the teacher, garbage
    collector and lawyer 241
Starr, Ken 225

T

Tarzan, and Jane 260–1
Tax Department 52–3
    and blondes 57
taxi driver, and naked woman
    257–8
teachers
    and St Peter 241
    and students 27
    and the maths class 245–6
tennis elbow 315–17
termites 34
theory, and reality 26–7
toothbrush 159–60
tuit 55
12 Days of Christmas
    e-mail version 99–102
    economic rationalism
        version 94–7
    politically correct 97–9

U

university
    and God 368–9
    life after 246–8
USS *Enterprise*, and light
    bulbs 300–1

V

vampires 43
ventriloquist 13–14
veterinarian 318–19
Viagra 273–4

W

WASPs, and light bulbs 301
Watson, Dr 407–8
weddings, Irish 309–10
what am I? 159–61
White House 213, 214,
    217–18
    ghosts 233–4
why did the chicken cross the
    road? 457–61
wife wanted! 304
wives
    and golf 163–4, 180, 183,
        200–1, 205
    and husbands 268–9,
        271–2, 333, 411
    and sex 252–3
    see also marriage
women
    and enjoyment of sex
        255–6
    and golf 176, 186
    and men 409–17
    and sex 251–2, 253–4
    and the family court judge
        310–11
    and the legless man 293

and the vacuum 304–5
domination of men 240
impressing 155–6
on men 153–4, 157
seminars for (presented by
    men) 157–9
see also blondes
words of wisdom 461–7
work 461
versus prison 88–90

see also employment; office
    life
working relationships, and
    the boss 82–4

Y

young executive, and golf 168